Trish Nicholson is ....opologist and conservationist, author of a range of non-fiction works, and a former columnist and features writer. She was born in the Isle of Man, gained her first degree at the University of Durham, and worked in regional government in Scotland and Europe before following a career overseas in rural aid and development, spending fifteen years in the Asia Pacific Region.

In 1998, she made a side trip to New Zealand on her way to Europe. What happened then set in motion events which, more than twenty years later, would result in the birth of a five acre forest and the writing of this nature memoir.

You can read more of Trish Nicholson's work and see more photographs and articles on the five acre forest on her website:

www.trishnicholsonswordsinthetreehouse.com

(where there really is a tree house) and follow her on Twitter

@TrishaNicholson

Passionate Travellers: Around the World on 21 Incredible Journeys in History
A Biography of Story, A Brief History of Humanity
Inside the Crocodile: The Papua New Guinea Journals
Journey in Bhutan: Himalayan Trek in the Kingdom of the Thunder Dragon
Writing Your Nonfiction Book: The Complete Guide to Becoming an Author

THE FIVE ACRE FOREST

TRISH NICHOLSON

Matador
9 Priory Business Park,
Wistow Road, Kibworth Beauchamp,
Leicestershire. LE8 0RX
Tel: 0116 279 2299
Email: books@troubador.co.uk
Web: www.troubador.co.uk/matador
Twitter: @matadorbooks

ISBN 978 1 8004 6487 2

British Library Cataloguing in Publication Data.
A catalogue record for this book is available from the British Library.

Printed and bound by CPI Group (UK) Ltd, Croydon, CR0 4YY
Typeset in 12pt Garamond Pro by Troubador Publishing Ltd,
Leicester, UK

Matador is an imprint of Troubador Publishing Ltd

All photographs were taken in the five acre
forest by the author and are copyright.

*For all tree-people and nature-lovers
and especially for MW, the pre-reader who provided the
final incentive
for me to publish this memoir when she wrote:
'I now feel the oneness with our planet like never before.'*

The Five Acre Forest
"Nature nourished them; it was here that they felt their deepest belonging and affinity."
John O'Donohue

CONTENTS

*Note: 16 pages of colour plates are
included just before Chapter 7.*

'Sand in my hair and between my teeth' – the
beginnings of my relationship with the wounded
sandhill that became 'the Dune'; its place in the
surrounding landscape among its 'cousins', the
dunes, lakes, swamps and beach; and my own
heritage of sand and trees.

'I was not the first to disturb the spirits of the dead'
– the burial place of ancient kauri forest beside the
Dune; kauri's special grandeur in fact and myth;
the history of its 'gold nuggets' of fossilised resin;
and present demand for the lustrous grain of its
exhumed timber.

'I can never take for granted the wondrous magic
of a seed' – the vulnerability and malleability of
sand as I clear noxious weeds; planting native tree
seedlings with the land's seasonal rhythm; the
nature of rain; and collaborating with nature's
networks above and below ground.

Zealandia

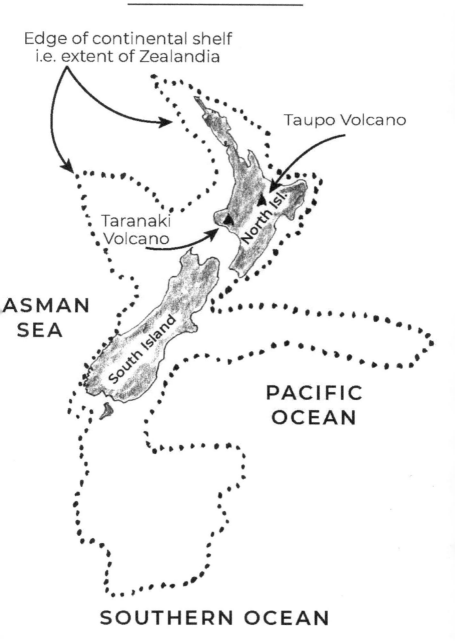

Edge of continental shelf
i.e. extent of Zealandia

Taupo Volcano

Taranaki
Volcano

North Isl.

ASMAN
SEA

South Island

PACIFIC
OCEAN

SOUTHERN OCEAN

Aupōuri Peninsula - Tail of the Fish

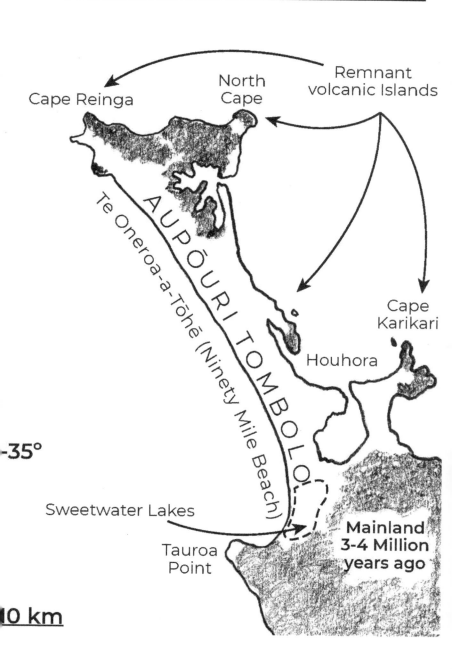

Northland Timeline

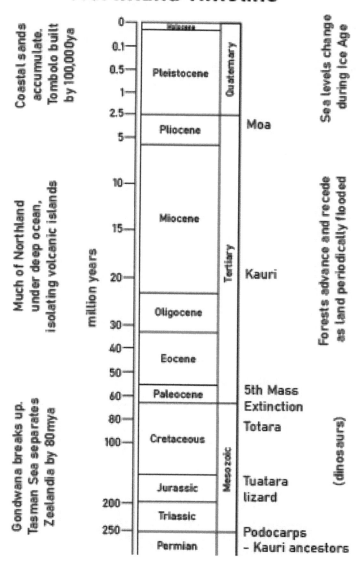

Coastal sands accumulate. Tombolo built by 100,000ya

Much of Northland under deep ocean, isolating volcanic islands

Gondwana breaks up. Tasman Sea separates Zealandia by 80mya

million years

0	Holocene	
0.1		Quaternary
0.5	Pleistocene	
1		
2.5		
5	Pliocene	
10		
15	Miocene	Tertiary
20		
30	Oligocene	
40	Eocene	
50		
60	Paleocene	
80	Cretaceous	Mesozoic
100		
	Jurassic	
200	Triassic	
250	Permian	

Sea levels change during Ice Age

Moa

Forests advance and recede as land periodically flooded

Kauri

5th Mass Extinction

Totara

Tuatara lizard

Podocarps – Kauri ancestors

(dinosaurs)

INVITATION

Planting a tree is an act of faith, an expression of hope in a future where the only constant is uncertainty. We may think of earth as immutable, a permanent foundation, solid ground beneath our feet, but every natural feature bears the heritage of its unique deep-time story which continues in transition. Into each landscape we etch our own lives, for good or ill, and write our own tales. You will find all of this within these pages celebrating place: the formation of the land, human history and mythology, and the physical and emotional practicalities of establishing native trees on an eroded, weed-infested sandhill, 'the Dune'. *The Five Acre Forest* is a story of transformations, of nature's generosity, and of personal fulfilment. It is a story of hope.

I met the Dune as a stranger while visiting the Far North of New Zealand. We were both migrants. I became an accomplice in healing its wounds, and am now more of a companion. This gives me time to muse and to write. Imagine that we are sitting on my veranda on top of the hill overlooking the lake. Strewn among the tea things on the table are a couple of sketch maps and a few pictures of trees, birds and insects, illustrations picked up from my desk to help me share with you the Dune's story.

CHAPTER 1

DUNE

Driving slowly, skirting a curve of the lake on our left, the estate agent pulls in to a flat rough-grassed area on the right that he wants to show me. 'It's been on the market for a while,' he tells me.

I had travelled around New Zealand several times before while on leave from working in Papua New Guinea and the Philippines. My latest contract had finished, and after spending a year researching Indigenous tourism projects in northern Vietnam and all over Australia, I was wending my way back to the United Kingdom, pondering future locations. I had no particular plans or goals in mind. After twenty-five years working in rural development, first in the Scottish Highlands and then in South-East Asia and the Pacific, a break was welcome. Past travels had taken me to South America, Africa, and Central Asia. Living such an itinerant life-style I had gathered neither lasting attachments nor dependants and felt free to explore new experiences and places. In this mind-set, a vague notion of settling in New Zealand had led me to contact the estate agent out of curiosity.

Flatness does not inspire me, but rising sharply from the grassed area is a slope masked in a mess of invasive weeds – gorse, elephant grass, and sundry woody shrubs escaped from early settlers' gardens – sprawling between patches of bare ground. And two long, open gashes run almost all the way down the slope bleeding loose sand scattering in the wind. Though oppressed and damaged, it is clear that this hump of land with a profile like an elongated cottage loaf, has never been domesticated.

I gaze at the wounded hill – a present moment, an instant out of eons transforming everything in time and space – and realise that I am looking at an old migrated sand dune. We are standing almost three kilometres inland from New Zealand's long sweeping north western coastline; its turbulent seas and prevailing winds create dunes that back the beach, their own slow migration now paused by human settlement and pine plantations. The coastal dunes are recent cousins to the dunes that surround the lake, trapping it within their embrace. The shapes of these lake-side dunes have long since been mutilated by bulldozers making way for buildings and orchards – except for the one in front of me, standing in mute expectation.

I, too, am a migrant; weary from life as a global nomad among communities who are working to heal old wounds, adapt to change, and grasp agency to avoid destruction in the new economic order. Farmers in villages built from the rocks to which they cling in remote mountain valleys; fishers in palm-wood houses thatched with reeds from the tropical rivers along which they cluster; herders in mud and clay dwellings as red as the wind-blown soils of their endless plains; and hunters in leaf-shelters deep in the forest: their problems in a modern world are myriad and complex. But they know that the solutions rest in their relationship with the land.

Working alongside these communities, I saw their engagement with the land went far beyond sentiment and livelihood. Theirs was a visceral attachment embedded in cultures that fashioned their psyche; myths and legends, like ligaments and arteries, roots and branches, couple their lives to land, water, air in all their manifestations. Nature occupies a living earth and people are an integral part of nature. It is the essence of Māori culture embedded in the surrounding landscape in which I stand.

And it is so in the Celtic part of my own heritage: the perpetual cycle of days, of seasons, of life renewed in place. At certain times and in particular conditions, free passage was possible between earth and the Celtic Otherworld – the timeless realm of spirits – forming the outer circle of time, of past, present and future. The spirits of past heroes pass through these realms bringing wisdom from earth's depths to the living. To me, this is symbolic of the complex life systems beneath the earth that transform death into new life burgeoning above ground.

The Nordic part of my heritage, too, echoes this rootedness within the earth, where Mimir, the keeper of the Well of Wisdom beneath the Ash Tree of Life extracts a cost for tasting the water. For one sip of this elixir of eternal insight, Odin, the Father of all the Gods, paid an eye. Life requires an understanding not only of what we see around us, but also what has passed beneath the surface and continues as an integral part of the whole process of living. The communities I have worked with understand this, espoused in a variety of ways in their own cultural traditions.

It is impossible not to be affected by this visceral attachment; not to share the bruising stress of maintaining the land's vitality, the wounds sustained in guardianship against forces seeking extraction rather than engagement.

I sense a growing kinship towards this scarred dune. And I have form with sand. Perhaps being born to sandy soils, on the small-holding where my parents scratched a living with a few chickens and goats in a straggling hamlet called Sandygate, set up a certain affinity, scattered the first grains of karma. We lived on the northern part of a small island, a couple of kilometres inland from the long smooth curve of the beach, the western side of a broad shingle spit formed of weathered glacial deposits and shaped by the Irish Sea. Or perhaps it was simply that mysterious intrigue of islands, whose dynamic edges hint at their secret histories.

Years later, the magical white beaches of Scotland's north-west coast called me to work on the *machair* – the grass plains beyond the beach that bind the sand in a protective blanket, nourishing the settlement of other plants. Maybe it is not a specific place itself that ties us, but the essence of a place that has become entangled within our psyche and whose elements may be found elsewhere. Where salted winds have travelled over immense seas; where the very foundations of the earth have been harassed and worn to grains of sand through unfathomable aeons; and bird-calls rise from trees and hills to echo between land and water. Everything is connected: what happens in one place tremors in another. The dune and I are both migrants, but unlike the dune, I am a stranger in this land, and yet it resonates within me.

But the estate agent is saying something, pointing to a possible house-site on that flat bit by the road, suggesting I cut away the lower part of the slope to make more room. I interrupt him, 'Let's go to the top.' He is reluctant, but follows my steep scramble through tousled weeds, avoiding the weeping gullies. The hill rises to about sixty metres and there is no path, since no prospective buyers over the years have wanted to venture on such a challenge to building.

Our exertions are rewarded by a pivotal view. To east and west, pastures spread across overlapping waves of lumpy sandhills, and a blue margin on the western horizon reveals a sea disarmingly tranquil. To the south, the small dune lake, a cobalt sky reflected in its glossy surface broken only by half-formed islands of yellow reeds. Beyond, a line of mountains, their silhouettes smudged in dreamgrey haze. Looking north, more hill pastures roll into a distant pine plantation. A few pine trees have strayed onto the dune's sun-facing northern side among a scattering of pioneering tea tree, but gorse has invaded most of the slope, too dense to let native plants establish. And some Australian eucalyptus trees have entrenched themselves, greedily sucking every bit of moisture from the ground. On this side, a thin brittle fibrous layer covers the sand beneath.

Between the dune and the rising grassy slopes is a strip of peaty wetland, described by the agent as 'an old kauri swamp': the burial ground of a whole *kauri* forest felled at an instant in some prehistoric natural cataclysm. Tiny insects remain trapped in the weathered resin of these ancient trees, prey to generations of treasure hunters – the 'gum diggers'. Millennia leak their secrets to the surface, drawing us into their story, though we are but a fleeting breath in the eternity of place.

I am already aware of the wider landscape that extends from this point to form the Aupōuri Peninsula: beyond the pine plantation, sandhills and occasional peat bogs and tiny lakes alternate for miles to the northern tip of the land – a hundred kilometres of narrow sandspit created by wind and sea over millennia. As shifting sands migrated eastward, they surrounded and partially covered a series of tiny rocky islands, joining them into one landform, a tombolo. The cliffs of North Cape, *Otou*, form the north-eastern tip, those of Cape Reinga, *Te Rerenga Wairua*, the north-western tip, like the two points of a whale's fluke. The features within my present view – the dunes, the swamp, the lake, the beach – each played a part in this prehistoric drama; characters in the story of the landscape's creation. Like cousins sharing genes from the same old sea-salt of a great-great-grandfather expressed differently in their individual personalities and careers.

Rain, ice and wind eroded New Zealand's primordial mountains, and rivers swept their sediments into the ocean; seas scourged the ocean floor, carried its gleanings on northward currents and threw up heaps of sand, pushing it across the beach with each high tide. Westerly winds sculpted the sand into dunes and pushed them onto the land. On the land, a shallow basin encircled by a gathering of dunes filled with fresh water and became a lake and, nearby, a small stream became blocked by dunes to form a boggy trough where the debris of vegetation over millennia decayed into peat. Migrated dunes, detained and released in turns by successions of migrant plants and climactic events, are now fixed in man-planted grass, pine plantations and avocado orchards. All over this landscape, ancient dunes nudge and over-ride each other in arrested motion, as if caught in a game of statues. But beneath my feet, this dune stands alone: slightly lopsided, the eastern side ending more steeply and abruptly than the western slope which curves down to flow into knobbly hills beyond.

Trapped inland among pastured hills, the dune is no longer viable as a sand-dune. To fulfil its destiny, to lead a long, full life in its new location and new role, the dune needs the diversity of native vegetation, the participation

of trees, bushes, climbers, ferns, mosses and grasses –
and an accomplice to plant and nurture them during
the early part of their journey. Pioneer tea tree – *mānuka*
and *kānuka* – fringe the swamp and edge the lake, but
nowhere else within my view are there other stands of
native plants: without a source of seeds for the wind and
birds to scatter, the dune cannot stabilise on its own. By
the time I skid and tumble back down the slope to the
estate agent's car, a gutsy breeze has blown loose sand
into my hair and between my teeth.

Showering and changing into clean clothes at the
backpackers, I realise I have stopped thinking about
other locations. The hump of sand has become 'the
Dune'. It insists on being part of my future, whatever
that future holds. But only ten days remain before my
onward flight to London.

By the time I leave for the airport, I have committed
to buying the Dune, and picked up a fat wad of
immigration forms. I own a tiny piece of a country in
which I have no right to settle.

The whole immigration process was tortuous because
of my wandering life – police reports required from
every country I had worked in, multiple documents to
prove my identity, endless forms for medical checks,
financial arrangements and currency exchanges to be
made – and it took a year of frantic activity to complete.
During that time, I made long-distance contact with the

planning office, and with a local builder the estate agent had recommended, while I made to-scale sketches of a small dwelling similar to the old settlers' houses that still dotted New Zealand's rural landscape. And for the first time in my life, I joined a gym to remain fit for the hard graft I knew was to come. Daily work-outs also helped to relieve the stress; I knew no one in New Zealand and was aware of the risks I was taking. Perhaps I was infected by the mood of momentous possibilities that was in the air during that first year of a new millennium.

When I returned to the Dune, I assembled my small building team, and arranged accommodation for myself in a neighbour's sleep-out so that I could supervise the project day-to-day. Ignoring neighbours' advice – to 'cut a good third off the hill's height to give enough flat area for a decent lawn' – I planned to build a single-storey timber cottage on low wooden posts on top of the Dune with the least possible disturbance to the land. Overlooking the lake in its kaleidoscope of moods and colours I have no need of lawns – frames to set off other man-made artefacts to best advantage when seen from outside. I am within, interested only in looking out to nature's own designs.

The low, one-room-wide cottage, aligned east-west like the Dune, is designed for looking out. Large windows and sliding glass doors on the south-facing side overlook the lake; the living area and my study open onto a veranda that runs the full length of the cottage. On the sun-facing northern side, smaller windows keep the rooms cool and another full-length veranda overlooks the swamp. My study takes up the eastern end where I am woken by the rising sun, not only in winter when it is directly ahead, but also in summer when it emerges a little to the south. There are no excuses for over sleeping.

CHAPTER 2

SWAMP

Between the Dune and the old *kauri* swamp is a gravelled lane running along the four-hundred-metre length of the swamp, before the lane turns sharply right to join the road that skirts the lake – the road that first brought me to the Dune. Timber and galvanised iron roofing sheets for the cottage must be brought along this lane, and a driveway must be laid from the lane to access the top of the Dune. We align it carefully along the Dune's contour because of the steepness of the slope and to prevent erosion. While workmen prepare the driveway, I step across the lane, duck between rusty wire strands of a fence and explore the swamp.

Black-winged, midnight-blue *pūkeko* – the native swamphens – flaunting white dabs under their tails, strut around on pinkish-yellow stilty legs like mechanical toys, thrusting red beaks into the earth to grab grasses and grubs. At my approach, they run a short distance over the tussocky ground and continue calmly feeding while keeping a wary eye on my presence. The shiny scarlet shields on their heads, like a flattened polished comb, bob up and down as their short strong beaks dig the ground. They step with confidence on extraordinarily long toes – four of them, widely splayed for balance on wet spongy surfaces – but dexterous toes with which they hold uprooted plants and insects while eating. In contrast to their smooth-scaled legs, *pūkeko's* knees are knobbly and grey, bringing to mind a skinny jogger wearing knee supports. I find it hard to take these birds seriously; their antics and appearance make me chuckle – coxcombs with attitude.

Accompanying this scene, concealed frogs and cicadas, and painfully felt hordes of mosquitoes, perform a noisy rhythm section of croaks, screeches and buzzings. The air feels thicker down here in warm damp stillness.

It is early summer after a wet spring. The ground is lumpy, disturbed by previous mechanised gum-diggings which have left it pockmarked with shallow pools and dotted with bits of broken tree roots, dark and dull when water-sodden, sun-bleached silver when dry. I hop from tussock to tussock, around dense reed patches, avoiding scratchy gorse bushes that have invaded the wetland. But one treacherous tussock is secretly floating; I end up knee-deep in black gunge – better described as thick peat juice than water – and sink my other foot attempting to gloop my way to solid ground without losing my balance. I fail. Sprawled full length, I fancy the *pūkeko's* alarm call is more of a shriek of laughter as it flies off into a nearby tea tree to watch from a safe distance. But literally face to face with the swamp, inhaling its fetid breath, the fustiness of antiquity, decay, and transformation, is the perfect way to appreciate its distinctive nature.

Regaining my feet, I see a patch of tea tree – pioneers on these poor acidic soils – has colonised the far edge of the swamp, dwindling part way up the sand hill pasture behind it. Further along the edge, a small plantation of fast-growing radiata pine has been planted and thinned for future timber extraction. I half close my eyes to focus my mind on how it must have looked long before human settlement.

In my imagination, I go back some fifty thousand years, to a time when our species had already migrated across south-east Asia and had settled in Australia; before the scattered islands and atolls of the Pacific were peopled; and long before the intrepid seafarers of eastern Polynesia arrived to colonise New Zealand some eight hundred years ago.

A time traveller, I stand at the far bank of the wetland. Behind me spans a trough of black water. Before me, a tangle of astonishing ferns and palms tremble in speckled sunlight; bright frilly fronds arching over still, silent water; some rise above their companions on erect tufted shafts, unfurling lace-patterned crowns like delicate parasols – and in the tufts, the pockets left by their shed fronds, more tiny mosses and ferns have anchored themselves; others drape their neighbours with long, deep-green strands, smooth, glistening, their supple stems invisible among this exuberance in air warmly bathed in spicy-musk.

Beyond the water's edge, on the rising slope, serried ranks of gigantic trees limit my vision beyond their massed and massive presence, their overlapping moss-bedraggled trunks. High and wide, they stand like Herculean columns. They are members of the podocarp family, ancient conifers which evolved hundreds of millions of years ago. I recognise most of them as *kauri* trees, with their top-knots of short thick branches pointing up into the sky. I must lean back, straining my neck to see their crowns merging into feathered remnants of morning mist that drift casually over them as if dusting them in desultory fashion. I push my way beyond the ferns, between the forward guard of leafy shrubs and small broadleaved trees, and into the forest.

Under the canopy, the atmosphere is claustrophobic. The screeches, squawks, whistles and trills of a profusion of flightless birds scuttering furtively through sparse low undergrowth and insects skittering everywhere are muffled by the density of vegetation. Everything is seen close-to in an eerie twilight – surfaces that glisten catch the eye first.

A step away, a huge grasshopper, its body the colour of polished copper and the size of a hamster, crawls over the stems of a creeper encircling a tree trunk. I recognise it is a giant *wētā*, a *pungawētā* – many different species of these flightless insects still live amongst us though the *pungawētā* is now rare. All around me, ferns, fungi, and epiphytes hang down from, thrust out of, or hold fast to, sodden lodgings attached to living plants, or among decaying debris in sinuous spaces between tree roots, and along dead rotting trees fallen against their brethren. And every niche, every surface, each millimetre, is a habitat for multiple invisible occupants. The forest is one heaving body pulsating with life.

A booming call ricochets between the trees, and the sounds of a heavy plodding shuffle through the undergrowth precede the appearance of two gigantic birds advancing in my direction. Their long thin necks are extended to reach leaves they tear with their beaks, but they stop to stare down at me with unruffled disdain. My eyes are level with the stomachs of their bulky, frizzle-feathered bodies borne on stocky legs broadening to amazingly fat thighs. From twice my height, they lower their small heads, forming a U bend in their necks, and peer at me in short-sighted fashion. Though birds, they have no wings, not even stumps of wings. They are giant *moa* and have no need to fear: the only predator capable of killing them is a huge eagle which patrols only the south island, not up here in the north. *Moa* thrived for at least three million years, gradually extending their territory in peace: all the different species of flightless birds are safe from predators. For the only mammals to evolve on these islands were bats of the air, and seals and whales of surrounding seas. I find the reason for this fascinating. I rest against a mighty tree trunk and revisit the story in my mind.

At the dawn of our present geography of continents and oceans – almost three-hundred million years ago – what were to become Australia, New Zealand, Antarctica and other southern continents were all part of the great plate of Gondwana. While unimaginable heat and pressure below the earth's surface began to break up this super continent, a slice of the earth's crust below the Pacific Ocean rammed Gondwana's eastern edge, thrusting up ridges and releasing volcanic eruptions. Over millions of years, this mountainous edge became detached and began a slow north-easterly migration, forming the new small continent of Zealandia, already clothed in podocarp forests. By about eighty-five million years ago, Zealandia was separated from Australia by the Tasman Sea and from Antarctica by the Southern Ocean. As Zealandia cooled, it started to sink until only a series of small low-lying islands would have been visible above the water.

In these islands' isolation, unique flora and a dizzying array of flight-less birds, bats, insects and reptiles evolved. If there had been any land mammals present at the time of that early separation from Gondwana, which is unlikely, they have left no trace and probably did not survive the fifth major extinction. That event occurred some sixty-five million years ago, when volcanic eruptions, possibly combined with a massive meteor strike, changed the climate and wiped out nearly half of the planet's vegetation and three-quarters of its animals, including dinosaurs. Although no dinosaur fossils have been discovered in New Zealand, many fossils of a contemporary marine cousin, an ichthyosaur – a long-snouted fish-lizard about three metres long – have been found, including one in the middle of North Island.

Forty million years after that mass extinction, the Zealandia continental plate beneath the islands started to split and the two parts began to swivel, colliding and sliding past each other, lifting the land, pushing up high ridges, and creating deep rifts amid earthquakes and volcanic eruptions. Those mountains have long since been worn down and replaced by others, as land was repeatedly submerged and thrust up again over millennia. The earth remains restive. New cycles of mountain building, erosion, and washing away of sediments into the oceans continue to shape a young landscape that is still 'becoming', in constant process of formation.

While I was in my deep-time reverie, the *moa*, having satisfied their curiosity, stomped back through the trees to continue feeding. But another observer has darted from cover. It stands rock still; a grey-green loose-skinned lizard about half a metre long, watching me with flashing glances. Perhaps suspecting a rival, he raises the centre ridge of his back into a line of threatening spines. But he is gone before I realise where he went. He is a *tuatara*, whose direct ancestors skittered warily around the crushing feet of dinosaurs on Gondwana, and already inhabited Zealandia when it drifted away. This canny lizard species was the only one of its kind to survive the fifth mass extinction and continue to the present day, though only in New Zealand. The *tuatara* is now rare, its numbers decimated by rats from incoming sailing ships. The trusting *moa* was even less fortunate: it had been hunted out of existence by the beginning of the fourteenth century.

A noisy tractor grinds along the hillside across my line of sight. My vision of the past fades. For a moment I feel abandoned, exiled. And yet, though the forest vanished, its past reality impacts the present, invisibly and visibly. The narrow swamp is an ancient peat trench, perhaps originally a stream locked in by the surrounding dunes which still hold it captive though now tamed and grassed for stock grazing – except on the south side of the trench, where the Dune which I intend to plant is the sole survivor; the others having been levelled and built upon.

For many thousands of years, this whole area was forested: shelter, larder and courting-ground for flightless birds, bats, reptiles and myriad insects. Neither wind nor sea has yet exposed fossil bones of any of the small or large species of *moa* in the dunes here, but their presence is almost certain, given the long occupation of podocarp forests that thrived in these poor light soils and sub-tropical conditions. Predominant among them was the mighty *kauri*.

Each *kauri* tree needs fifty years to develop into its mature shape, takes eight hundred years to reach its prime and full height of up to fifty metres, and can live for up to four thousand years. The largest known *kauri*, documented in 1860 near Waipoua forest and nick-named Kairaru, measured twenty metres around its girth, and thirty metres from the ground to the first branch. Although *kauri* growth rates vary during their long lifetime and so there is no exact relationship between size and age, Kairaru was so huge that it could have been over three thousand years old. Unfortunately, we will never know for sure, because on 4 January 1898, the tree was destroyed in a forest fire during a severe drought.

Since my misspent childhood, hiding up in trees to escape the unfathomable adult world, I have been in thrall to the ancient tree-lore of my own Celtic-Norse heritage. From the Druid's sacred groves of oak trees to the runic Ogham script – the esoteric language of ritual and myth – trees were sacred dwelling places of spirits and central to Celtic lore. Groups of Ogham runes were often linked to significant places and objects, including wells, rivers and birds, but Tree-Ogham was the largest and most important division; it is said that the birch tree was the first symbol used by the inventors of the runic script. In time, twenty-four different tree and shrub species represented letters in the runic alphabet, including alder, ash, willow, hazel, whitethorn, holly, heather and gorse as well as oak and birch. In pre-Christian Celtic traditions, trees bore the essence of life and the spiritual force of all living creatures above and below the earth in nature's eternal cycle.

In Nordic cultures the sacred ash tree, Yggdrasill, was the Norse Tree of Life at the centre of the cosmos, whose roots encompassed the Nine Worlds of the natural and spiritual universe. Beneath its roots sprang Urðr, the Well of Wisdom. Among the many stories surrounding Yggdrasill is the description of Odin, the Allfather, chief of all the gods, one-eyed because the price he had to pay for drinking at the Well of Wisdom was one of his eyes. In another story, Odin hangs from a limb of the tree for nine agonising days: the acquisition of wisdom requires sacrifices. It is still the custom in many parts of Scandinavia to plant a tree in the centre of each field in the belief that it will protect the planter's family and bring good fortune. The trees are carefully nurtured – for them to die would be a worrying omen of misfortune. It is significant that, in the many myths featuring Yggdrasill, it has a mortal existence as well as a spiritual one: the tree needs protection and care for it to survive. For the death of the sacred ash tree heralds the coming of Ragnarök, the decline of the gods and the end of existence. A startling prescience as we now experience the implications of destroying the earth's forests.

With such a background of tree-lore, I was keen to discover the *kauri's* place in Māori mythology.

In the final phase of creation, when light and life emerged from the great restless darkness, Ranginui the Sky Father, and Papatūānuku the Earth Mother, held their many sons between them in such close embrace that they felt smothered. The children asked their strongest brother, Tāne, to separate their parents to let air and light into the world. From his position curled up like a germinating seed between his parents, Tāne braced his shoulders against Papatūānuku's ample flanks, placed his feet on Ranginui and, straining to stretch himself to his full length, slowly pushed Ranginui out into the sky. Tāne became the *atua* or divine spirit of the forest embodied in the mighty *kauri* that appears to hold up the sky above the earth; his children are the trees, ferns, birds and insects that flourished in their new freedom.

Ranginui's tears of sorrow at the separation from his partner flooded all the land, and one of Tāne's brothers, Tāwhirimātea, was so enraged at the pain caused to their parents that he left his siblings to join his father in the sky and became the *atua* of weather – we will feel his anger later, when we go to the beach.

The ancestors of *kauri* first evolved long before Zealandia broke away from Gondwana. *Kauri's* small thick leathery leaves look like oval scales; when attached to the trunks of its juvenile form they point upwards giving the tree an archaic, almost reptilian appearance. The *kauri's* endurance through millennia of floods, earthquakes, volcanic eruptions, fires, climate changes and even the fifth mass extinction, is hard to grasp. It's enough to send anyone hurtling face down into a swamp. And some forty thousand years ago, this particular wetland was a scene of devastation for the surrounding *kauri* forest.

Whether as a result of flooding, storm or some other natural cataclysm, *kauri* trees fell en masse like a ranked army of lead soldiers tipped off a table. Those that fell into the peat trench were preserved in the wet anaerobic conditions of the swamp. Over time, forest debris was washed down from the hills and covered them with more peat to a depth of eight to ten metres. Exploring the swamp, I was staggering about on top of an ancient arboreal burial ground – there is sadness in that. But I was by no means the first to disturb the spirits of the dead.

In many parts of upper Northland – the limited range of the tree's natural occurrence is north of thirty-eight degrees latitude – groves of *kauri* collapsed in response to some environmental trauma at different periods, some as recent as a thousand years ago. More commonly, natural deaths over centuries overlaid each other accumulating in the same place. Since migrating from Polynesia early in the thirteenth century, Māori had collected bits of ancient *kauri* and nodules of *kāpia* (gum) that had worked to the surface – gum is good for kindling the cooking fire – and carved *kauri* timber into *waka* (canoes). But two distinctive features of *kauri* trees led to a modern cause of their devastation, both the living and the dead, generated by European settlement and the industrial revolution.

The bole of a mature *kauri* is smooth and straight, retaining its wide girth for up to twenty or thirty metres. As a juvenile, a rikker, long thin leaf-laden branches radiate from the trunk at close intervals all the way from the base to the top, draping into a cloak of leaves that generate energy for its massive growth. But once a *kauri* has been growing for about twenty years (in tree-time they are still children), they begin to shed lower branches and small discs of expanding bark, a process that continues for another thirty years. In a particularly satisfying example of nature's recycling, the tree's shallow upper roots feed on this accumulated debris decomposing around its base.

The second feature is that all parts of a *kauri* exude resin – which is different from the sap that rises from the roots through the tree to nourish its limbs and leaves. The resin is a turpene oil that hardens to heal and protect the tree's outer wounds. *Kauri* increase their resin production as they begin to shed their juvenile branches and bark over decades, leaving only a pattern of flat scar patches and shallow stretch marks on the mature silver-grey surface. Resin dribbles down the trunk and accumulates into hardened lumps that drop onto the forest floor and may be washed by rain into swamps and rivers, sometimes ending up on the beach.

The clean bole of living *kauri* delighted lumber jacks – though felling such a girth was not easy work with a double-ended hand saw. And long lengths of knot-free timber with tight grain delighted the milling and timber merchants, the builders, and the exporters. Because *kauri* do not taper towards the crown, their timber yield is greater than for any other species. And though a conifer and therefore classified as a 'soft-wood', *kauri* is the hardest of its kind, its slow growth ensuring that woody cells are tightly packed together to form a close grain. The rings on a tree stump record each year's growth: the closer the rings, the more slowly the tree has grown.

Massive trunks, misleadingly called *kauri* 'logs', were dragged out of the forest on skids pulled by teams of up to twenty oxen straining at their yokes. If there was a river nearby, logs were slid from the bank and floated down to the mill. Since few stands of *kauri* remained on the Peninsula, main felling operations were south of the tombolo in areas of larger population. As tools mechanised and transport developed, so did the rate of felling; by the early twentieth century, only some five per cent of Northland's original *kauri* forest remained. The early settlers must have gazed up at the mighty forests and assumed they were an infinite resource, a mighty gift of Providence – much as the massive Amazon forests have seemed until recently. Only those who live within them, and whose lives depend upon them, have understood the necessity to nurture and conserve forests.

In the wetlands and peat bogs, it was the *kauri* tree's resin – the gum – that first attracted the attention of the industrialising world, to feed its growing demand for oils to make varnish, paint, polish, oil-cloth and linoleum. Much later, the hardest, clearest pieces were worked as jewellery, enhanced by the fact that *kauri* gum can be any colour ranging from the palest golden syrup to black molasses.

After poking about on the swamp's fringes, I find a knobbly, wrinkled-looking opaque lump just beneath the surface. It fits neatly into my hand. On any other stretch of ground I might have passed it over as a long-dead shrivelled potato. But here, I recognise it as the outer crust of weathered gum. It is hard but brittle. I flake off the crust at one end with the penknife from my pocket.

The inside resembles clouded glass containing tiny streaks and specks and is the colour of fine-cut marmalade. It looks like amber but it is not fully fossilised as true amber is – a process that takes millions rather than thousands of years – *kauri* gum is much softer and generally less clear. I am reminded of childhood visits to the seaside at Whitby, on England's north-east coast, where I would fossick along the shore for bits of jet, one of which I still have in an old biscuit tin of treasures. Jet, too, is a relatively soft, pre-fossilised resin, from the 'monkey-puzzle' tree – *Pehuén* in the Mapuche language of its native Chile – a fellow member of the genus Araucariaceae and early ancestor of *kauri*. The voices of eons whisper to those who listen – it takes my breath away.

I scrape the outer crust of the gum nodule with my thumbnail and test it with my tongue: the taste is tart and powdery. On my hands, the gum leaves a dank, slightly nutty, oily odour – an attic smell – the sort of smell that greets you when you open the door of a piece of antique furniture that has been closed for years. And my imagination conjures a bulky wardrobe somewhere in Victorian Britain being polished by a maid using furniture oil made with *kauri* resin.

Initially, Māori families would camp around the wetlands for a season of digging gum with hand tools, selling the lumps they found in the towns. Such small transactions continued for some seventy years before a surge in demand attracted migrant workers, many from Croatia, who eked out a harsh livelihood living in primitive shacks for years at a time. In all weathers, they probed the spongy ground with long steel gum-spears to locate buried trees and hardened chunks of resin. With spades and pick axes, they dug pits as deep as two graves to retrieve lumps of gum that might weigh a few ounces or a couple of pounds – occasionally, a lucky strike of near a hundredweight would be found. Those who could afford it, wore long rubber boots; those without sloshed about in pits of black peat sludge up to their knees, groping for the treasured nodules until their arms were as black as their legs.

Between diggings, the accumulated heaps of gum nodules had to be washed in sieves, scraped, and bagged for visiting buyers to inspect, weigh and offer their meagre price. Many local men took out licences to work the gum fields, either alone or with their families. Migrants more often worked in digger gangs of eight to ten, pooling their efforts and dividing their earnings. On pay-out day, anxious diggers gathered around the rough-timber crossbeam where the buyer hoisted each bulging hessian sack of gum onto the hook of a simple lever scale with its heavy brass counter-weight, while his lad entered the measurement into a notebook. Sometimes the scale was simply suspended from a pole resting on the shoulders of two diggers.

In her family memoir, *Mount Camel Calling*, Alice Evans notes that it was not the diggers in the gum-fields that became rich, but the few local buyers and traders who bought the gum, and the Auckland export merchants to whom they sold it. And as the same few buyers often owned the land, and the stores that provided tools and food on credit, a good chunk of a digger's earnings returned to the buyer. Some migrant gum-diggers eventually saved enough to return to Europe or to buy a plot of land locally and recruit a wife from home; others died of fatigue and sickness. The rush for gum was so intense that people dug the beach for washed out lumps, and even bled living trees, gouging the bark and collecting the resin when it had run out and congealed; a risky enterprise for the collectors clambering up the sheer sides of the trunks, and for the trees which often died from multiple wounds.

Later, on larger diggings, mechanisation took over some of the operations as stockpiles of gum were processed in huge warehouses by company employees. At that time, the long-dead trees themselves were of no value to the industrialising world; sometimes they were blown to smithereens with dynamite to scatter the resin and make it easier to collect.

Once cheaper synthetic substitutes replaced natural resins, the gum trade dwindled, but the prehistoric swamp timber now drew the attention of the marketplace. Though still fine-grained, timber from the ancient species is more figured with whirls and ripples than that of living *kauri*. When sanded and oiled, its honey-gold sheen catches the light like shimmering silk and satin. Having been preserved for thousands of years in anaerobic conditions, unless carefully dried and sealed, the timber cracks and rots outside in the air.

But properly treated and finished, it became popular for fashionably unique and expensive furniture.

In addition to the draw of the wood's beauty and great antiquity is the fact that this *taonga,* this natural treasure, exists nowhere else in the world. There is perhaps no greater irony than that the heaviest overseas demand currently comes from wealthy Asian families intent on burying their venerable dead in coffins of forty-thousand-year-old *kauri* wood – perhaps in the hope of their preservation for a similar span.

Swamp *kauri* is a treasure to the scientific community too. Palaeoecologists' studies of preserved wood, leaves, cones, pollen, gum and underlying soils in several ancient sites is providing data on *kauri* growth with vital clues to environmental changes over a continuous record of almost four thousand years – a scientific asset rare anywhere else on the planet.

Part of the swamp in which I stand has recently been dug with a small excavator to extract the ancient *kauri* wood, so the estate agent told me. A mobile mill had been set up at one end to saw the logs into planks – a small operation from which the wetland is already showing signs of recovery. (Sadly, its future would turn out to be quite different.)

Peat juice has soaked through the seams of my old hiking boots that served so well on dry mountain scree. With wet feet, I squelch back from this first of many visits to the swamp, inspired anew to plant young *kauri* on the Dune's northern slope overlooking their ancestors' graveyard.

CHAPTER 3

DUNE IN AUTUMN AND WINTER

Here in the southern hemisphere autumn begins in March. During autumn and winter the sun hangs low, seeming to orbit the Dune. Rising through a silver filigree of pre-dawn haze in the east, it reclines into a bed of old-gold, spreading a carmine-hued duvet over the sky in the west; each in turn reflected across the mirror of the lake, completing the circuit.

Each morning, I marvel at the random revelations of a rising mist carrying with it the pre-dawn fragrance of damp freshness like new leaves. Later in the day, I gauge the wind's strength by herds of tiny white waves racing like lemmings across the surface of the water. I no longer wear a watch. My time is paced by shifting light and textures of water and vegetation as, slowly, I learn the shapes and needs of this my chosen place.

Autumn heralds the start of the wet season. Rain. Such a diversity of trauma and tranquillity is contained in that little word. Sometimes, the tenderest touch, little more than mist with intent, a lover's breath on the cheek accompanied by sunshine – what the Bhutanese call '*metok chharp*', 'blossom rain'. The very air luminescent, enchanted. It is a good omen; the time for rainbows. I view this soft rain as the caress of Ranginui Sky Father in his sorrow at separation from Papatūānuku Earth Mother, while the fine morning mist rising from the ground is her loving response.

Tiny round leaves of coprosma bushes glitter like diamonds; the drooping branches of *rimu* trees hang and drip in long wet tresses. Soft rain on smooth sand glistens like wet skin before it is welcomed by a thirsty soil. And this gentle caress prepares the ground to absorb another rain: the bruising, wind-whipped deluge whose clattering din across my tin roof drowns all other sounds within. Outside, it rattles the big glossy oval-dinner-plate leaves of *puka* trees, bending them to pour water from their tips onto the plants below, and cascades down tree trunks to penetrate to their roots. Though most of the rain draws in from the west, the heaviest, fiercest winds and rains storm in from the north-east.

During one June cyclone, wind screamed through door frames in fury at being denied access, while the whole house trembled on its sand base. The storm raged all day, slim trunks of cabbage trees bent over in submission, their long narrow leaves all straining in the direction of the wind as if an aggressive hand was dragging them by the hair. I must have forgotten to latch the bedroom window firmly because, in the middle of the night, a gust caught the edge of the window frame and tore it from its hinges, flinging it into the bushes below. I spent the rest of the night trying to hold down the blind to keep out the worst of the wind and rain. By morning, Tāwhirimātea, the weather god, had vented his anger, and an innocent dawn beamed on my weary world.

These onslaughts would gouge the sand but for the thick mulch layered to break their force. As most native species are evergreen, there is no communal shedding of leaves to dance to the tune of autumn breezes. The blaze of gold from evening sun heightened by a darkening sky is restricted to the reed beds in the lake. At first, I find this absence of a familiar seasonal marker disturbing; as if a segment of the circle is missing, a slice cut out of the year. But each tree and shrub follows its own cycle of leaf death and renewal, growth and rest, responding to soil moisture, air temperature, and its natural intuition. Even conifers replace their needles in rotation every few years. Dropped leaves, last year's spent flowers and emptied seed pods fall to the ground, and I tread down dead bracken to add to the protective layer over the sand to break the force of heavy rain, delaying its onward rush sufficiently to seep into the earth. When the first rains fall onto scorched ground, the air fills with the odour of wet ash, of slaked thirst – deep breaths bring a sense of relief, of release from the stress of drought.

The wet season transforms the colours and textures of everything. The sand glows honey gold instead of parched blonde; tree bark reveals deeper, richer shades, intricate shadows giving depth to their grooves, niches and secret places. Discs and traceries of intricate lichen are highlighted against darker shades of bark, looking like clusters of dry crisp blue-white snowflakes; mosses and tiny ferns congregate in damp crevices; and elegant fungi colonise shadowy spaces above and below ground, their necrophagous preferences completing the transformation of death's debris into nourishment for the living. Among my favourites are the thick white strands that form a perfect spherical open-work basket, and the stubby bright-red cylinder, edged around its open 'mouth' with a fringe of fine filaments like a sea anemone that has lost its place. Nature is a mathematician in her precision and an artist in her creativity.

Not until years later, after reading Peter Wohlleben's *The Hidden Life of Trees*, did I understand fully that fungi seen above ground are only the showy bits, flamboyant entrances to a vast subterranean system of transport, supply, and information transfer. In the darkness below ground, fungi spread long traces, mycelia, from one tree root to another and beyond. Attached to the fine hairs of tree roots in a million tiny nodes, fungi and tree live in a relationship of symbiosis: a partnership of exchange and reciprocity for mutual benefit. While sunlight empowers green plants to produce sugars through photosynthesis, symbiotic fungi feed on these sugars from the roots — their only source of sustenance. In return, as the fungi transform decaying matter, they draw water and nutrients from the soil into the roots of their partner plants and can protect them from other harmful fungi and bacteria. As in all relationships, there is no 'free lunch': up to a third of the sugars a tree produces via photosynthesis may be consumed by its partner fungi. But it is even more complex.

Of the many fungi species, each one may be attached to many trees of the same species, and each tree may host many kinds of fungi. Beneath the forest floor, the reach of interdependences and interconnections is vast. Communication throughout this massive underground network operates by the passage of chemicals and electrical signals involving far more than mutual feeding; it enables trees of the same species to communicate with each other. Although natural scientists have long been aware of underground connections, researching the details takes many years because of the long life of trees and therefore the timescale of measuring the mutual effects of reciprocity between fungi and plants.

This interdependence between below ground and above ground means to me that darkness and light are not a duality but a system of reciprocities. I am reminded of ancient wisdom: of the Celtic Otherworld below the earth and its role in perpetual cycles of growth, death and transformation; of Norse cosmology where the roots of Yggdrasill, the Tree of Life, are both nurtured and threatened from below; and of the interrelatedness of all living things which is the foundation of Māori world view. When we disturb the earth, we disrupt vital networks sustaining life above the soil. I try to disturb it as little as possible.

My own seasonal rhythm favours clearing pernicious invaders during this cooler, wet season. And damp ground is firmer; I cause less damage to the surface when scrambling up and down the slopes, following the contours of the Dune's curves to avoid erosion – its constant vulnerability. Gorse bushes – the 'furze' of nineteenth-century literature – chest-high and picturesque hedging in their native Scotland, run rampant in this sub-tropical climate where they can grow into small trees of three or four metres. If native seedlings had begun to establish between them, I would have left the gorse bushes a while longer as sun shade and wind shelter, but they grow too densely and draw too much moisture out of the sand for seedlings to flourish. I leave a few bushes to shield sites where I intend to plant but the rest must be removed. Their rigid stems rear mockingly over my head as I approach to hack them back and lay them down to rot, to return their life force to the soil. It will be a continuing task: everyone seems to delight in telling me that gorse seeds remain vital in the ground 'forever'.

But other, beneficial seeds have also lurked in the ground waiting for the light: tiny leaves emerge on the surface and grow into tangled native coprosma bushes with tough wiry stems and tenacious orange roots; and dark green fans of stiff native grass stalks develop into long arching blades so sharp they are known, with good reason, as 'cutty grass'. Both coprosma and cutty grass help to hold the sand in place; and they colonise so freely, they will soon need to be checked from smothering newly planted seedlings.

Rough clearing work binds me to the Dune. Sand embedded beneath my nails, dirt encrusted in the creases of my hands, and smears of blood from cuts and scratches all seem symbolic of my growing bond with the land. Everything is returned to the earth in sustainable cycles akin to social reciprocity: a two-way exchange. One-way extraction denudes the soil as, socially, it diminishes the soul.

Escapees from the gardens of early settlers who tried to recreate their homeland – a natural ambivalence of migrants – have also run riot in this environment and become noxious weeds. They smother other plants, preventing native species from regenerating, and disrupt the natural ecosystem: jasmine, ivy, buddleia, wild ginger, cotoneaster, periwinkle, privet, pretty lantana, poisonous woolly nightshade, pampas grass – a prized decor specimen in Europe here pushes out the graceful local *toetoe* – and keeping them out requires constant vigilance. These are the worst among fifty or more other introduced invasive plants that have had centuries to spread their seeds and rhizomes and which it is now illegal here to produce and sell. They still abound in private gardens though, by intention or neglect. People seem fond of their lantana shrubs with their clusters of bi-coloured pink and yellow flowers and are reluctant to weed them out; a fondness that surprises me because, when disturbed, the plant gives off a truly noxious, acrid odour that penetrates the skin and lingers on clothing for days.

It is not the fact that they are not native plants that matters. Many introduced or naturally migrant plants have contributed to gardens and managed environments. The problem is that the delicate balance of forest, woodland and wetland ecosystems is disrupted when species from elsewhere become dominant and reduce local diversity. Because they have no natural predators in New Zealand, introduced animals, such as possums, rats, stoats, multiply and spread prodigiously; they actively destroy the environment by browsing on forests and killing native birds.

Writing up the account of his visit to New Zealand on the *Beagle* in 1835, Charles Darwin notes the devastation caused by many British species, not only rats from visiting ships – including his own, no doubt – but also plants not always entirely innocently brought into the country. 'In many places I noticed several sorts of weeds, which, like the rat, I was forced to own as countrymen … the common dock is also widely disseminated, and will, I fear, forever remain a proof of the rascality of an Englishman, who sold the seeds for those of the tobacco plant.'

All living trees are the most generous of nature's providers for humans as well as for birds, animals, insects, and often, for other trees. They offer medicine chests, food pantries, nesting sites, resting places, anchors, shelter, shade, leaf mulch and, on the Dune, lookouts from which kingfishers guard their burrows in the banks below and herons watch the lake. But introduced species from Australia have become troublesome – particularly eucalypts (called 'gums' in Australia) and wattle trees – initially recruited by farmers wanting fast-growing windbreaks. Eucalypts have learned to suck so much water from the soil to store against the frequent droughts in their native habitat that other trees are starved out from the Dune: when a eucalyptus tree is felled, water pours from the stump and cut limbs. And wattle trees seed so profusely that carpets of seedlings sprout up for years after the parent has been removed. Wattles are such a menace that they must all go, but I leave a few eucalypts and pines at strategic locations where they provide shade and their underground communities can remain intact, perhaps able to nurture new seedlings when I plant them.

I hired an arbourist to fell the larger eucalyptus trees and pines, but for other clearing and planting there is only my own labour and hand tools and I need to pace myself. One of the earliest tasks was to establish paths and steps for accessing the slopes without damaging them. They are cut after rain: only wet sand holds its shape long enough, like building sandcastles on the beach – or dreamcastles on the Dune. Paths are edged by round timbers to hold the sand until vegetation stabilises them. Steps are simple: a length of wood as a riser held firm by wooden pegs is all that is necessary; my perpetual walking will tamp down the tread. Paths are narrow, skirting the slopes; steps curve around contours.

I start at the top of the slope. Each step must be angled slightly into the ground to encourage water to soak in otherwise it will become a scouring waterfall in heavy rains. I kneel to hammer in the wooden pegs but still it is a back-breaking job. This phase is a labour of years: a small section cleared for planting and a few metres of paths settled each season. Eventually, they will form a circuit linking east, west, north and south.

People on neighbouring properties think I am mad, a crazy immigrant. 'You'll never do it,' they say. Nevertheless, several offer practical help for a while. One with a bench saw cuts timber into step lengths for me and puts points on the pegs. He also arranged for a group of friends to erect a short length of fencing and a wooden gate across the flat rough-grass area alongside the road to stop truck drivers pulling in to use it as a comfort stop. Another, with a mini-digger, dug out an area at the top of the drive to house the garage-cum-potting shed and nursery space. And a local farmer dropped off some bails of rotten hay for mulch. For some months, I collected droppings from the fields of an emu farm which saved the farmer from doing this necessary chore while adding nutrients to my ground. Or so I thought, until I realised that I was scattering grass seed everywhere I did not want it.

The Dune is all sand. Not a single rock. And I introduce none, nor mans' mimicking metal. All the work is in wood, arisen from the soil that will, in time, redeem it. Nothing is straight, nothing flat: it would be an imposition. But paths are necessary to navigate this curvaceous land, to tend needy plants, to discover the micro destination best suited for a particular plant, for its roots to travel, to interact successfully with complex networks out of sight below the Dune's surface – for us both, a process of discovery through trial and error, of tolerating uncertainty, and awaiting results. It is a delicate balancing act.

The sand's malleability reminds me of the brain's plasticity. Sand-forms change, seeking equilibrium under the forces of wind, water and gravity. A sand environment thrives best with plants responsive to its natural qualities and histories, as my capacity for understanding expands within the parameters of my own psyche. I, too, can expunge oppression and heal past contusions. And as the work progresses, my vocabulary expands with every hammer-blackened thumbnail and wrenched muscle.

The less strenuous activity of raising plants during this season is a welcome relief. It is a contemplative task. Some native shrubs and small trees grow well from cuttings of firm new growth in the early autumn. One neighbour at the far end of the lane shares my enthusiasm and grows native plants in her small garden; with her advice I snip bits off a range of the many species of coprosma, corokia, and hebe, dip their stems in a rooting solution, or in honey, and keep them damp in a fine gritty growing mix in the shade house.

Not all of them will take root, of course. Despite my anxious vigilance, there are many reasons for failure: changes in temperature; too much or too little moisture; the stem not as matured and self-sufficient as it appeared when taken. And it may take several weeks or even months before a cutting begins to grow on its own new roots. My moods swing between jubilation at the successes and disappointment at finding sadly drooped or shrivelled sprigs on my morning rounds.

Many of the faster-growing trees self-seed readily, and I go further afield to scout for seedlings of *akeake*, *matipou*, *mahoe*, lacebark, five-finger, *whau*, and *kōwhai*. The seedlings of these pioneering forest edge and lower storey trees are easily recognisable even at a few inches tall, unlike some forest trees, such as *kauri* and lance-wood, whose juvenile forms are completely different and may persist for ten years (forty years for *kauri*) before beginning to transform into their mature shape.

On fine dry days, I collect seeds from mature pods of ground-cover plants and grasses before they burst and are distributed by wind and birds. The thin shiny-black seeds of flax, *harakeke* – as long as my thumbnail but half the width – tumble from sun-blackened pods arranged a score at a time on stiff stems, rods held up like banners two metres above their long strap-like leaves; the tiny black, flattened round seeds of *rengarenga* lilies shaken from grey-dried brittle stems, each bearing a dozen or more small seed pods where the starry white flowers had been. I place them in re-cycled milk cartons of fine seed mix to germinate alongside the cuttings in the shelter of the shade house.

A narrow strip of levelled ground alongside the garage-cum-potting shed has become the 'nursery'. Shade from intense summer sun is more important than heat in our mild winters, so the need is for a shade house not a greenhouse and I erect one from a kit. Shelving I construct from narrow strips of old roof irons supported by columns of building-blocks – rough and ready but sufficient. Once seedlings have grown strong enough to be re-potted, they join the ranks of other rooted youngsters in the lines of triple-parked seed-trays along the nursery strip.

The surface area of the Dune is approximately five acres: averaging the planting distances of different species, and allowing for desirable plants already growing here, up to eight thousand plants – ranging from small grasses to ground cover plants to understorey shrubs to forest trees – will be needed to cover the area. At the peak of production, my little nursery holds up to seven-hundred plants and seedlings growing each year, all needing to be watered once the sun has retired for the night. A simple repetitive task; I would like to describe it as my evening meditation, but in truth, it is often accomplished while half asleep from the fatigue of a day's work, even while being eaten alive by mosquitoes.

There are times when I feel overwhelmed by the task I have set myself and what has to be done to achieve it; both the things that I can control and the more significant impacts that I cannot.

Even when tired, my spirits rise when I watch seeds sprout into life. To change their form from that first exciting pale hoop of stem or minute green leaves pushing up through the soil, to standing upright, bearing their first and, for some, second sets of leaves as if recognising their identity in stages – living their story one millimetre-sentence at a time. However many times I bear witness, I can never take for granted the wondrous magic of a seed.

Take the *pōhutukawa* tree, for example – the tough, rough-barked tree whose showy crimson flowers in December gained its nickname as our Christmas tree. *Pōhutukawa* thrive close to the sea where they withstand dry conditions and strong salty winds, stabilised by a crown up to thirty metres in width like a beflowered wide-brimmed hat. Their seeds develop in a tiny round green cup the size of a small pea, grooved into thirds where the cup splits open when brown and ripe. I tip a split cup onto the palm of my hand and realise that *pōhutukawa* seeds are smaller than lettuce seeds. And yet, in each minute brown speck is the complete formula for a tree that can grow twenty metres tall and live for eight hundred years or more. Theirs is an astonishing story. How does one deal with such feelings of awe? I let the tiny seeds trickle across my palm and I laugh: because of their illusion of simplicity, and because, tiny as they are, they tickle.

Indeed, there is something truly awe inspiring in planting a forest tree. While living in the Scottish Highlands in the 1970s, I planted an oak sapling; it was little more than a metre tall. Over the years, the property had changed hands, but I visited the garden twenty-three years later. The house was unoccupied and I wandered like a ghost through the shrubbery between the house and the lane until I found that planting spot on a little knoll. To my great delight, I looked up into a healthy young oak tree more than three times my height.

My hope is not only to stabilise the Dune while producing a natural source of native seeds, but also to create a sanctuary and food source for native birds. For this, I need a wide range of shrub and tree species providing nectar, fruits and seeds at different seasons. Some of the best food larders are forest trees such as *pūriri*, pigeon-wood, *miro*, *tōtara* and *rimu* – and all will become habitats for tiny creatures and growing things that begin to fill out the intricate life of a forest. I am aware, too, that a well-working forest will take at least a hundred years to become an effective ecosystem; there is no way of knowing what may happen during that time or which species will flourish in the long term. My project is an act of faith; like all such acts, it needs to be strengthened with practical backup – another reason for planting as many different species as are likely to cope with the conditions. A critical requirement for most native plants is freely draining soil. That, at least, I can provide. I take risks, pushing the range of some species; there will be failures, but also unexpected successes.

Most forest trees are slow to germinate and grow. I would be underground myself before I could raise enough ready to plant. And apart from occasional specimen trees, there are no native woodlands left in the surrounding area, so I order saplings up to a metre tall from a specialist nursery that sources seed from this region – of course, I order young *kauri*, too.

I soon discover that trees thrive best when planted

small, when they have less body to maintain and can focus their energy on sending their roots to explore their new setting, on finding their way into life-supporting partnerships below ground. Smaller saplings also need less supplementary water during their first few summers than taller ones with more stems and leaves to support. Although many species prefer poor light soils and should not be fed additional nutrients, *rewarewa* for example, they all need initial watering to establish and grow.

This is especially important on the Dune, not only because rain drains so quickly through the sand, but also because, in the absence of existing native woodland, the supportive fungal community below ground will take years to develop. Newly planted saplings must depend on their root hairs to absorb water; they may put on negligible top growth for several years while they extend their roots in all directions to sustain them for the long term. It is best that they do: over-optimistic spurts of new growth may wither and die during dry months, so I water them sparingly – enough to keep them alive and healthy, but not so much as to dissuade them from the necessity of developing root systems that enable them to seek out and store moisture for themselves in the future.

Regular rain can be expected to start from mid-May or June. As soon as the sand remains damp enough to hold my hand-print, I prepare to plant the seedlings, rooted cuttings and young saplings that are ready – this gives them three or four months of winter and early spring rains to help them settle in place.

At the beginning, I had to recondition my mind to the seasons being 'upside down'. My inner graphic of the year's progression had to be reversed, like my orientation to the land: south facing is now the cooler slope catching winds originating in the Antarctic; north facing receives the sun all day, whether the high sun of summer or the low sun of winter. The northern hemisphere's summer solstice, when the tilt of the earth brings the longest day of sunlight to the north, is our winter solstice, the tilt placing the southern hemisphere in the shade of our shortest day. While Celtic cultures celebrate Beltane on the evening of June 21st (a new Celtic day began at sunset) with purifying bonfires honouring the power of the sun, here it is not the shortest day that is most significant but the season of Matariki, the Māori New Year and, traditionally, the time to plant *kumara* or sweet potato.

The dates of Matariki, around June and July, vary each year because they are set by the Māori lunar calendar and are determined not by the sun's passage, but by the configuration of the stars: by the first rising of the open cluster of the Pleiades for which Matariki is named. The Pleiades are young stars – only a hundred million years old – still glowing sapphire heat. Being among the nearest stars to the earth, they have been observed and accounted for in various ways in most cultures of the world for thousands of years, probably since our prehistoric foraging forebears. As stars were the principal navigation aid to the Polynesian seafarers who first settled on these islands, it is not surprising that the stars' configurations, along with the lunar calendar, should be a more prominent presence than the sun in their myths and seasonal rituals.

There are more than one thousand stars in the Pleiades cluster, but only the seven most lustrous – widely known in the rest of the world as 'the seven sisters' – are usually visible to the naked eye. They are characterised in a popular Māori story as a mother surrounded by her six daughters. Matariki and her daughters arrive each year to visit their *kuia*, their grandmother, the Earth Mother, Papatūānuku. Each sibling brings a particular quality to assist Papatūānuku in maintaining the health and strength of the earth's plants, creatures and water sources during the coming year: qualities of understanding, kindness, generosity, endeavour, and caring – attributes that are taught as desirable human virtues in our relationship to the environment and to each other.

Discovering Matariki gave me an unexpected and welcome link to my own cultural heritage – 'upside down' of course, but familiar. In the Northern hemisphere, the Pleiades are visible for most of the winter, but are at their highest point in the sky during November, and were associated by the ancient Celts with the rites of Samhain, celebrated according to the lunar calendar during October and November. These rites marked the transition from the light period of the year just passed, to the dark period to come, and were symbolic of the transformation from life to death. Faint remnants of this festival remain in the modern celebration of Halloween, though largely stripped of deeper cultural meaning.

Samhain was the beginning of a New Year for Bronze Age Celts, as Matariki is for Māori.

But it is not only the celebration of the beginning of winter in their respective hemispheres according to the stars and the lunar calendar that links Matariki and Samhain in my mind. There is a deeper cultural affinity. The cold darkness of a northern European winter held real dangers of starvation and disaster for struggling agricultural communities. The Druids, in their wisdom, identified each star of the 'seven sisters' with a human virtue that would help their people survive the winter: truth, kindness, patience, purity, temperance, faith, and determination. During the midnight rituals of Samhain, Celtic priests exhorted their congregations to live by these seven virtues, as Māori myth encourages their people to live by the virtues of Matariki and her six daughters. Our human fragility binds us all through our shared earth, sky and sea.

If regular rain comes earlier, I do not wait for Matariki – one year, during a particularly wet autumn, I could begin planting with confidence in mid-April. But I found some useful guidance in the Maramataka, the traditional Māori lunar calendar. Interest in the Maramataka to determine optimal times for planting, harvesting, fishing and other activities has increased in recent years as part of a wider revival of Māori culture and language. We are close enough to the sea for the lunar pull of the tides to affect the high proportion of water in all living things; some have even suggested that the level of nectar in flax flowers along the coast responds with its own tiny tides. Certainly, the *tūī* birds seem to think so: their visits to the deep funnels of flax flowers at different times of day seemed haphazard, until I noted the times and realised that they seemed to visit more often during high tides.

In Irish Celtic traditions, Áine, the moon goddess, reigned over fertility as well as love, and influenced the productivity of crops and cattle – the main sources of livelihood and prosperity. In one of many myths about Áine, she is the daughter of Manannán mac Lir, the sea god; in another she is his wife. Either way, it is not surprising that the moon and the sea would be in close association. The moon's gravitational pull on earth's water is stronger than that of the sun because of the sun's far greater distance from the earth.

Lunar influence on vegetation has long fascinated those who support sustainable living and seek to engage as closely as possible with the earth's natural rhythms. According to a popular calendar constructed especially for New Zealand gardeners, the time between the new moon and the first quarter is most favourable for leaf growth; from the first quarter to the full moon is the best time for sowing seeds and planting crops to bear fruits, flowers and seeds; from the full moon to the last quarter favours growth below ground for root crops, trees and cuttings; and from the last quarter to the new moon is a barren period, best for weeding, composting and cutting timber for fuel.

I have not tried to test any of this by planting at different times and comparing the results, but my intuition assures me that it is a reasonable way to organise working the land. If other conditions like soil moisture and my time schedules fit, I take cuttings and plant saplings and seedlings between the full moon and the last quarter, and focus on clearing and mulching between the last quarter and the full moon. I need all the help I can find: if I can recruit the moon to assist my endeavours I will not pass up the chance.

The one-year ecology course I opted for as part of my first degree opened a door to an intriguing world of wonder, inspiration, and endless questions. But when it came to the practical side of planting, I learned more from the forest-dwellers and subsistence farmers I had worked with in Asia and the Pacific. Theirs was the wisdom of generations in adapting to often rugged land and extreme weather.

Preparation begins by alleviating the steepness of the ground as far as I can. I dig planting holes that tilt slightly back into the slope so that the roots will not grow too near the surface, and the sand around the plant must be saucer shaped and well mulched to hold water until it soaks in, rather than running off and eroding the slope. If the ground dries out for a prolonged period, especially on the north-facing slope which is more fibrous, it becomes hydrophobic: it resists water initially and so takes a long time to penetrate. Finally, I anchor the front of the planting hole by pegging partly submerged lengths of old timber in front of it. For this, I forage in the swamp across the lane, and over old *kauri* diggings on the land of a nearby friendly farmer.

There is something particularly satisfying in the idea of ancient *kauri* limbs and roots cradling a new generation of young trees, especially when the youths in question are their own descendants. It may seem fanciful to imagine there would be any recognition between the new growth and the ancient wood, but chemically, there might be. Living *kauri* grow hefty roots deep into the ground to anchor their great stature, but they feed from shallow fibrous roots which, with the help of fungi, draw nutrients from the decaying debris of their own fallen leaves, bark and cones that collect around them. Over time, this recycling of their own chemical structure creates a soil around them too acidic for other species and acts as a deterrent to competition, including competition from their own offspring which are rarely found beneath their parents.

I plant each tree species in small groups of three or five; folklore advice is that trees grow best this way because they 'like each other's company'. But there are sound ecological reasons too: it will encourage the formation of the underground fungal network that transfers nutrients and other chemicals from the soil into the trees' own circulatory system, linking the roots of a group of trees, enabling them to provide mutual support. In the future, water, plant sugars and other nutrients will pass, via fungal networks, from older trees to their young offspring who bear fewer leaves and less deep roots to source their own needs. The Dune, entirely sand as it is, offers a challenging environment to many species; they need all the help I can provide. Over the years, they will reciprocate by creating a more complex soil around themselves which will help other plants to establish within their shade and shelter.

Clearing and planting often takes much longer than it should. Working on the north-facing slope I gaze over grassed sandhills and the wetland, favourite haunts of swamp harriers. Their wingspan extended to their full metre width, they glide in from the hills, sweep back and forth over the swamp, then swoop in decreasing circles to a final dart for their prey. If the prey escapes, they begin the whole performance again. It is impossible not to linger, watching, until a harrier has secured its dinner. And a mob of cattle – beef steers being fattened – roam hungrily over the pasture, seeking grasses long enough for their tongues to grasp and pull free (sheep, in contrast, nibble short grasses with their teeth, but there are no sheep kept on these hills). When the mob congregates at the top of the hill, I know to expect rain. With luck, it will be the perfect gift from Sky God, Ranginui, a gentle watering of my new plantings. But if the sky darkens and glowers, more likely is the gathering rage of Tāwhirimātea to send a scourging storm rain.

From the south slope, I am all too willingly distracted by my constant companion, the lake. Each time I glance across, something is different. The air, the colour and texture of its surface, the movement of reeds – each creates a capricious feast of fluidity. Even on a still day, a gentle air current may riffle the polished surface of the water to smoked glass.

Our winters are mild, rarely dipping below ten

degrees centigrade even at night. I have occasionally seen an early morning light frost on the grass verge along the road below, but never on the Dune. Vegetation continues to grow during the winter because there is regular rain: lower than usual rainfall in winter indicates a summer drought to follow because the ground begins with a moisture deficit. Bracken, the native fern, *rahurahu*, may grow to two metres or more during winter, and if it will provide light shade for struggling plants during searing summer heat, I let it grow; the rest I cut in spring and trample down as a mulch to conserve moisture in the soil for as long as possible.

This native fern (*Pteridium esculentum*) deserves a special mention: though now considered a pernicious weed by many stock farmers, bracken carries an ecological and cultural history as complex as its root system; controlling its presence is a tricky balancing act. Bracken's deeply buried rhizomes from which roots and runners spread in all directions, make it virtually indestructible, even by fire, especially in our sub-tropical warm and sandy soils where wind-spread spores from the fronds' under-surface easily germinate and dig-in. Their tightly curled fronds push up through the surface of spaces opened up by fire or other causes of forest removal, and though bracken was present in many parts of the country before humans arrived on the scene around the early thirteenth century, it has since become almost ubiquitous as a result of subsequent land and forest clearance. For early Māori settlers, the starchy rhizomes were also a staple food. In the account of his

1835 visit, Charles Darwin referred to 'the tyranny of fern' which he saw everywhere he went.

Ecologists point to the importance of conserving bracken in a controlled way, not only as part of cultural history, but also viewing bracken as a long-term precursor of natural reforesting: while its root networks hold the soil and prevent erosion, emerging trees will become dominant because bracken 'is suppressed by even moderate shade.' But I have not found this in my experience on the Dune. Where I have planted, bracken shoots emerge from beneath tree saplings, pushing up long rigid stems for two to three metres through their branches to over-top them, where the opened fronds eventually shade out the young trees if not removed; and incidentally compete with saplings for water. My balancing act with bracken must allow it to continue stabilising the soil, yet conserve soil water, and enable only the right degree of shade during the hottest season.

While northern Europe cuts Christmas trees and builds snowmen in December, we bask on the beach in summer sun. No one has an appetite for steaming plum puddings and roast turkey. But European settlers would not be denied their traditional Christmas dinner. They enjoy two Christmases: gifts and the long summer holiday in December and January, and dinner in the coolest part of the year, in July. Even after four or five generations and much blending of Māori and European (Pākehā) families, the custom is still followed that many clubs, institutions and major employers hold their

Christmas Dinner parties in July. No such thing as too many opportunities for good food and cheer.

During wet stormy days that punctuate our winter, I snuggle down beside my woodstove to review the progress of my project and plan for the future. Plans are always tentative because nature is the boss. I am merely an assistant. I am short-circuiting plant successions by selecting species and adding nutrients, water, and shade not yet available to them in their pioneering role, but it is a false vanity to think that nature can be rushed. I must bow to her imperatives. The Dune teaches me to be patient; to work with the rhythm of its heartbeat deep below my feet. And as the years pass, the deep gullies, the weeping wounds, are healed with new growth.

CHAPTER 4

LAKE

That first fateful day driving around the curve of the lake, catching a glimpse of sparkling water and golden reeds between the trees was delightful, but the experience in no way prepared me for how I would feel living at an elevation overlooking this body of water.

The road passes the lake, revealing no further sparkling glimpses on its way to the coast. But a footpath wends through the band of tea tree and occasional cabbage trees and tree-ferns that surrounds it, making a complete circuit. For only a short part of this distance is the view open across the water, and here, seedling trees have been planted to grow for the future. Vegetation surrounding the lake is important to absorb impurities washed down from the surrounding agricultural and residential land that might contaminate the water with artificial fertilisers, herbicides and other chemicals. The lake is without inlets or outlets such as springs or streams, only the balance of evaporation and rainfall draining from the surrounding sandhills determines the level of water and concentration of chemicals that affect the lives of its plants and other inhabitants.

In the rainy season, the peaty path becomes muddy and waterlogged, but in dry conditions the walk takes about an hour at a steady pace. In my first few years here, I was inundated with houseguests. Some of these overseas friends had not contacted me for twenty years, until they wrote claiming my hospitality. Pleasant though company is, for a semi-recluse it can feel like an invasion; in the early evening, rain or shine, I would send them off along the path to give me an hour's peace to prepare dinner. And I would do the circuit often enough myself.

Walking around the lake shore, tracing its subtle indentations on a path of soft tree debris and surface roots, I am under a cool canopy of sable-green light; the water a tantalising glimmer occasionally visible between the trees, beyond the undergrowth and edging of reeds and rushes. It brings to mind those awkward moments at social functions when someone you are intrigued to know is barricaded around with other people, and you are uncertain of how to meet them, or even what to say when you do. But from the top of the Dune, the lake is transformed.

I gaze down into an almond-shaped eye. A perpetually open eye, fringed by feather-topped *mānuka* and *kānuka* trees. The circle of tiny islets and reed beds in the centre, gold-specked in sunlight, I imagine as the eye's iris. And the gentle curves of overlapping hills and mountains on the horizon like an arching eyebrow. Sometimes they are little more than an indigo smudge in an evening haze or the faintest outline veiled in a rheumy-eyed morning mist. At other times, their facets and gullies are starkly sculpted by a forensic midday sun that reveals all secrets. This Maungataniwha Range in the distance behind the lake rises to almost eight hundred metres; rugged remains of primeval volcanic rocks erupted from the ocean floor and thrust up over Zealandia in eons past. If I were a bird, these forest-clad mountains a forty-kilometre flight away would be a favourite place to cruise.

At either end of the lake, taller trees – pines and eucalyptus – preen themselves in the water's reflection when the light is bright. And, unceasingly, night and day, the sky looks into the lake's eye and sees itself there. The sky's crimson flush at sunrise and sunset paints the water pink; when the heavens are cerulean blue, the lake sparkles as a sapphire; dark thunder clouds turn the water to beaten lead, rain stippling the surface; and at night, the moon tip-toes across a darkly glistening path of polished obsidian. As I write this, a train of small fluffy cumulous clouds chugs slowly across the sky from west to east; they, too, paddled across the water until a few minutes ago when a frisky breeze ruffled the surface to opaque glass, making the lake's eye inscrutable.

When we look into another's eyes we seek their honesty, and their recognition of our own truth. We see the presence, or absence, of mutual trust. It is uncanny how we can manipulate our body language and faces to give the impressions we wish to portray, yet our eyes reveal all unless we look away – and that movement, too, is revealing. It seems we can only close these windows; the view within cannot be disguised when open. Even an expressionless, dead-eyed look tells a story. For lovers, the deeper search is between souls whose intimate gaze replaces the ambiguity of words.

Sky and lake have no secrets from each other, no pretences. My gaze probes for understanding of the lake's true nature and its past, and encourages my own self-honesty: Wordsworth's 'harvest of a quiet eye, that broods and sleeps on his own heart.' I am reluctant to look away. Whatever I am doing, my glance returns constantly to the almond eye beneath my window, and each time it will have changed in texture and colour – especially colour, in a multitude of hues: blues, greys, greens, hazel, violet, clear or sparkling, marbled or veiled. And colour impacts our feelings and thoughts. The artist, Wassily Kandinsky, gave a percussive description of this effect: 'Colour is a means of exerting a direct influence upon the soul. Colour is the keyboard. The eye is the hammer. The soul is the piano, with its many strings.'

The hues of the lake play upon my mood. During occasional dense mists at the change of the seasons, when the lake disappears completely and nothing but an opaque pearl void exists beyond my veranda rail, I am conscious of an aching absence. The lake's presence has become a necessity to me as it is for my fellow creatures, though for different reasons.

I watch a slow-winged heron strain into the air

extending her neck towards the shimmering water and plunge like a long-handled dagger to spear her prey. A little sacred kingfisher, *kōtare,* darts from his burrow, pauses on an overhanging branch, eyes twitching to peer through the surface, and in an iridescent flash-splash-gulp, he is gone. Ours are a different colour to the European kingfisher; they wear a priest's white collar with a pale apricot surplice under their metallic-turquoise jacket.

Pūkeko plod ponderously along the muddy shore, feeding before returning to their nests among the reeds. And the dragonfly hovers and skitters leisurely over the murmuring waters as if time were of no consequence. The lake has seen ages of time and all of it of consequence. Time and tides created it, for it is a rare dune lake, an example of a special ecosystem sadly dwindling worldwide – and it is a cousin to both the swamp and the Dune.

The lake was formed by a process similar to the swamp: a hollow in the land left by encroaching dunes, perhaps trapping a small stream or simply collecting run-off from surrounding slopes. But it is a much wider, shallower basin than the swamp trench. The lake extends for about fifty hectares (over a hundred acres) and is little more than six metres at its deepest point; the sediments beneath the lake bed are much deeper, deeper than is presently known. But, you might ask, if this is a bowl of sand, how has the water not drained away? I saw a clue to the answer one very dry summer.

We had received no rain for weeks while a relentless

sun battered the ground. Evaporation was so high that the lake's edge receded some twenty metres from the shore immediately opposite the Dune, exposing mud flats that are normally under water. One day, I noticed what looked like a huge slab of wood buried in the mud, its surface water-planed and polished. It was an old *kauri* tree fallen thousands of years ago.

Kauri and other conifer forests grew in this area before the lake was formed. Encroaching sand might have smothered the trees, or the gradual accumulation of water in the basin between dunes could have waterlogged the roots and killed them. Whatever environmental trauma caused their downfall, the trees had grown here for thousands of years like those beside the swamp, and their unique interaction with the soil explains why water accumulated instead of draining away.

Kauri trees, along with other podocarp species, thrive in acidic, sandy conditions. The sand in this area originated from eroded mountains and volcanoes of central North Island, and the sediment, swept along northern sea currents to create our beaches and dunes, consists mostly of silica (quartz, ground glass) but also traces of aluminium, iron and magnesium which the trees process and shed as organic material during their long life-cycle. Over millennia, rain leaches these organic minerals out of the soil, freeing them to percolate down where they accumulate and consolidate into an impervious layer, a hard, uneven pan of varying depth which may be several metres below the surface. Podocarps, among the planet's oldest genus of trees, give their name to this process: 'podzolization', creating podzol soils; it is this hard pan that holds the water of the lake, as it holds the water of the swamp and the aquifer beneath the ground along the rest of the Peninsula.

Recently, researchers extracted a continuous core of material from the bed of the lake. The core sampled only to a depth of six metres, but at that depth it captured sediments laid down about fifteen thousand years ago – an indication of how slow nature's processes can be. The transformation and adaptation of life and land forms, though sometimes violent and immediate, at other times almost imperceptibly gradual, is nonetheless constant. It is true in our own lives; adaptation is the only way to survival.

Each layer of the core recites an episode of the lake's life story. Bands of silt – compressed remains of the lake's plant and marine life – alternate with layers of sand laid down by the passage of newly migrating dunes; ancient pollen grains show *kauri* forests emerge, disappear and reappear, replaced temporarily by that of beech when the climate cools. Analysis is still incomplete and a much deeper core would be necessary to trace the lake's earliest memories and the probability that, at least once, it vanished under migrating sands, later to be reborn.

The recumbent *kauri* trunk I saw in the mud that dry summer – hidden quickly after the rains – could be as old as those in the swamp. Swamp and lake are separated only by the Dune; they are connected below ground by the water table held above the pan. And the almond-eyed lake is not alone: other, much smaller lakes still survive among the pine-planted dunes between here and the sea. But over millennia, dunes and lakes, like forests, come and go. Only the broader time-frame can suggest when the lake was born.

Why am I so fascinated by the lake's origins? The mystical element of water, the absolute necessity of life, has been recognised in all the world's cultures; spirits or special powers abide in wells, bogs, rivers, springs, seas and lakes. Water sources were often sacred sites defined by specific gods and rituals in the ancient Celtic world of my heritage. Their belief in the healing power of moving water, that it could repel the passage of evil spirits, is reflected in later times in the health benefits of spas to dispel sickness. But not all water spirits are benign. Imaginations anxious about what lurks unseen beneath dark waters have created extraordinary mythical creatures in folklore: Fossegrim, a Scandinavian water sprite who seduces women and children with the music of his violin and draws them under the water to drown; and the *bunyip*, skulking in Australia's outback waterholes and swamps, waiting to eat humans who stray too close.

In one of the older Norse sagas, the lake of Amsvartnir (literally: 'as dark as pitch') is terrorised by the wolf-monster, Fenrir, until the gods capture him on the lake's Lyngri Island. Such stories were frequently depicted in Viking carvings and runic scripts on rune stones – prominent rocks and memorial slabs – and it grants me irrational pleasure to recall that a warrior vanquishing Fenrir with his spear is still visible on a partially eroded, tenth-century rune stone known as Thorwald's Cross, on the Isle of Man, not far from where I was born.

Not unexpectedly, given Iceland's dramatic landscape and challenging climate, a water monster plays a central role in Icelandic mythology too. The Well of Wisdom, the source of all life that feeds the roots of the sacred ash tree, Yggdrasill, is guarded by Mimir who is wise in ancient lore because he drinks the well's water. But the well is also the abode of a villainous serpent, Níðhöggr, who chews at the tree's roots. Nothing has changed but the vocabulary: the planet's sources of life are still threatened by villainous gnawing greed that only the acquisition of wisdom can overcome.

Taniwha, spirit creatures of Māori mythology, may inhabit caves and forests but are more often to be found prowling in rivers, lakes and other dark watery places. Lake Tikitapu, near Rotorua in central North Island, is one of four lakes formed by lava flows in an ancient volcanic crater where, in times past, the local people were preyed upon by a well-known *taniwha* named Kataore. From the description of Kataore, he must have resembled a *tuatara* as big as a dinosaur. The story relates how he lived in a mountain cave about three thousand feet above the western bank of the lake. Around the lower, eastern shore, a shady path led under overhanging trees like the path around the almond-eyed lake. It is here that Kataore would wait, hiding among the trees before pouncing on passers-by and eating them. But he went too far when he devoured a chief's daughter along with her attendants. The chief sent a party of a hundred crack warriors to rid them of the monster. Potent chants, *karakia*, were recited to subdue Kataore before the warriors mounted to his cave, fastened around his neck a rope made of flax leaves and, with enormous effort, dragged him out into the forest. Kataore had recovered some of his energy by this time and a fierce struggle ensued, but the warriors finally killed him.

Such stories contain different layers of meaning. They may be metaphors for other forms of struggle and embody tribal history and cultural knowledge, but they also reveal the intricate bond between people and landscape, and especially the significance of water. Many similar tales describe different ways of trapping and killing *taniwha,* but the creatures' personalities vary; many are protective and benign – unless they are aggravated – because their principal role is to safeguard sacred sites. Other stories name friendly *taniwha* who accompanied the first canoes or *waka* of Māori Polynesian ancestors on their journey from legendary Hawaiki, believed to be the islands of Tahiti (earlier named by Captain James Cook the 'Society Islands'). Sometimes a *taniwha* would guide the leading canoe or guard the canoes after landing.

The *taniwha* that inhabits the almond-eyed lake beside the Dune must be of a benevolent nature to yield up the lake's treasures without penalty to humans. In a centuries-old tradition, the lake's golden reeds – actually a species of sedge, the *kuta* or *paopao* – were the favoured source of fibre for weaving mats and water-proof cloaks because their tubular stems grew longer than in other lakes. During my first few years on the Dune, I watched the harvesting which took place in autumn, between April and August, when the reeds were matured. Divers cut the stems as close as possible to the root – a rhizome, like a tuber it will put up new shoots in the spring – and float them to the surface. Strong healthy stems, well over a metre long, were gathered into bundles and canoed to the shore. *Kuta* is rarely harvested in this lake now, although it is still used for weaving a variety of craft items.

Sometimes, the exploits of powerful *taniwha* are traditional explanations of landscape features: according to one story, Lake Omapere was formed by Waihou (a *taniwha* whose mother had come with the first canoes from Hawaiki) when he thrashed his tail back and forth creating a shallow depression. But for a deeper understanding of the almond-eyed lake, I need a different kind of story.

In a rough arc around the lake are at least eight other, smaller lakes and patches of swamp trapped among dunes of widely different ages. All are roughly three-kilometres from the beach, and became known collectively to European settlers as the Sweetwater Lakes; no doubt because, despite the closeness to sea and sand, they are freshwater lakes, useful sources of water for humans and livestock. Māori refer to this area with a more poetic description, 'a land of floating islands, moving hills, taniwha, and heroes'. To wander among these small lakes casts the mind back through eons of time. Some may have been linked to each other in former days, or were larger lakes divided by encroaching sand.

And a fascinating clue to the constant transformation of this mutable landscape is the presence among a common fish species of an intriguing genetic variation.

The tiny silvery *inanga*, the smallest of the whitebaits, is found in most fresh-water sites near New Zealand's coasts. But it appears, from early and as yet incomplete research, that *inanga* in the almond-eyed lake carry in their DNA a genetic trace from a much older marine species, indicating that, long ago, the coastline was much nearer to the lake than it is today.

The slow accumulation and migration of sand that formed the tombolo of Aupōuri Peninsula could not have begun until around two million years ago. That was when the northern section of Zealandia was thrust up for the last time above sea level to become the landmass of North Island. In the sea beyond, scattered rocky islands were now surrounded in shallow water rather than the deep ocean as they had been before, and they would eventually be joined together by migrated dunes. Sea-washed sand would have begun to accumulate against the rocky northern edges of the landmass. The process has been continuous: dunes overlaying dunes, but age can be roughly estimated by the extent to which old dunes have stabilised themselves, their sand grains and mineral traces consolidated.

Exposed remnants of cemented dunes from one to two million years ago have been found on sites where the original landmass coastline would have been, a little to the south of the Sweetwater Lakes. An early, narrower tombolo was likely completed by about a hundred thousand years ago. During that time and since, sea levels rose and fell; dunes and lakes, like the forests, appeared, disappeared and reappeared.

The shallow, six-metre core taken from beneath the bed of the almond-eyed lake captured only the last fifteen-thousand years; intriguingly, the researchers found sandstone beneath the sediment. A deeper core could reveal its true antiquity. Until then, the lake hides her years in a shimmer of ageless beauty.

Walking along a truck-wide forestry track westward, between the Sweetwater Lakes and over pine-clothed dunes towards the beach, I pass ghosts of the recent past. An open, flat area between dunes, once a wetland where *pūkeko*, duck, frogs and lizards foraged among its reed beds and ferny fringes, is now an impenetrable mass of gorse bushes too dense for native plants to gain a footing. Last century's gum-digging and subsequent draining of the wetland left it uncultivated; the poor soil and ruined land abandoned.

A similar pattern is repeated on one side of the track and then the other; some were once small lakes, others peat bogs. The vegetation that now fills them depends on how thoroughly the land was drained in the past and the density of shade as the pine plantation grows around them. I catch sight of some tall ferns away off the track to my left; heading for them, I pick my way between the trees, wary of tangled kikuyu grass. This perennial, sun-worshipping invader scrambles over everything to a height of a metre even under the pines, and its name – *Pennisetum clandestinum* – is appropriate. Long, creeping feathery stems weave a loose mat wickedly concealing old tree limbs trimmed and dropped at all angles. When I'm lucky, the unseen branch I accidentally step on is dead enough to break and let my booted foot crash through onto firm ground; if there is a spiteful *taniwha* lurking, my leg is caught between two branches and an ankle wrenched as I fall, cursing, onto spiky twigs and bruising knobbly cones. Today I am lucky.

I reach my goal and realise the tree-ferns mark the edge of an isolated remnant of wetland that is rapidly deteriorating. Overwhelmed by invasive weeds and plantation shade, it is unable to maintain itself. And further away in a more open clearing what, at first glance from a distance, I think is a small meadow of waving grass heads, turns out to be a lake completely choked from edge to edge in *kuta*. It seems the reeds have not been cut for generations – perhaps their quality is poor or they do not grow to a length that pleases the weavers. This tiny dune lake is following a natural trajectory, colonised by plants which, if left undisturbed, may form a small swamp, or dry out sufficiently to support tea tree and, eventually, other trees which will replace the lake.

I crash and stumble my way back to the track; I will continue along it to the beach another day. In the meantime, I sit on a stump amidst a monotony of dark overbearing pines and muse on the local history that spawned this maimed landscape around me.

It is not only the landscape that has suffered. The local economy in these windswept sand-lands has ebbed and flowed like the sea, taking a toll on people as well as the environment with each new tide of prosperity or poverty.

Archaeological studies suggest that at the time of the first human inhabitants arriving from Polynesia – about eight hundred years ago – rolling sandhills were stabilised by vegetation. Ancient *kauri* and other conifer species were far fewer than during past climates and sea levels, and were joined by broadleaf forests such as *pōhutukawa, pūriri, karaka,* and *kohekohe,* with tea tree, shrubs, and grasses forming marginal scrub – all species that I am planting on the Dune. Sufficient forest clearing and burning – though not always intentional – had been practiced by the first Māori inhabitants for Captain James Cook, in 1770, to note the western shores in his log as 'a desert coast', and for his botanist, Joseph Banks, to describe it as 'almost entirely occupied by vast sands'. It is worth noting, though, that these were observations through a spy glass from the decks of *Endeavour* – they did not land on the west coast and likely underestimated the extent of vegetation further inland.

After the arrival of significant numbers of European settlers in the mid-nineteenth century, burning-off scrub and clearing trees began in earnest; first to create grazing for livestock, and then for access to gum fields. The demand for *kauri* gum promised prosperity for the Far North, though primarily for a small number of gum buyers who held monopolies. Initially, the gum was dug by Māori families for whom few other sources of cash income were available. The prices offered were low, and they were hardly much better at the peak of the trade when Croatian migrants accounted for the majority of gum diggers. At the height of the market, over seven thousand diggers were engaged in gum extraction in the Far North.

The wetlands and dune lakes of Sweetwater, including the swamp behind the Dune, became one of the four most productive gum-fields along the Peninsula. At peak production, Sweetwater gum-fields employed at least two-hundred diggers and, as there were no roads, two miles of railway were laid to take gum to the Awanui River for onward steamer transport to Auckland.

Sitting on a tree stump in the still, silent pine plantation, it is hard to visualise the teeming activity of diggers; the trundling rattle of the train; the squeaking axles and hollering drivers of bullock wagons plying back and forth; and the noisy conviviality around clusters of *nikau* palm and canvas huts at the end of a working day. There was a touch of the 'wild west' in these pioneering settlements where people worked hard, played hard and drank hard. As well as the local store and canteen owned by the gum buyer, entertainment was offered in the tavern cum dance and billiards hall – in one account, run by a formidable woman more than capable of keeping the men in order.

But the balance of natural forces that had taken so long to form the landscape was put out of kilter; the sand-lands were too fragile to withstand the onslaught. Clearing of scrub and trampling by livestock exposed the dunes to strong westerly winds and cyclonic storms; before the end of the second decade of the twentieth century, reports of 'the sand drift menace' were a regular feature in the local press. Pastures, fields of crops and even entire farms were inundated by wind-blown sand; almost half the tombolo had become shifting dunes. Intermittent small scale attempts to bind the sand by planting marram grass had little effect.

In the meantime, large high quality lumps of *kauri* gum became harder to find, and in any case, the industrial world began to use synthetic resins. Despite a partial revival of trade when small chips of lower grade gum were exported to make linoleum, the market was declining. Week after week in the newspapers, the government was urged to buy gum in order to help 'distressed gum-diggers.' Before much could be achieved, the Great Depression of the 1930s took effect in New Zealand; unemployment increased everywhere, and urgent meetings held up and down the Peninsula talked of potential 'starvation' if no relief was given.

The government set up a land settlement scheme to encourage small dairy and beef-fattening farms, and road building and other public works provided employment while improving transport for farm products. Old gum-fields, though deeply pitted and soured, were drained along with other wetlands for farming. Around Sweetwater, wetlands and swamps with their native wildlife disappeared almost completely.

And where did all these pine trees come from? Previous efforts to stem the 'menace of drifting sands' had failed; new farms and drainage schemes were continually threatened, and when sand began to clog the roads and disrupt business in the towns, the problem could no longer be ignored. The government Forestry Service, normally focused further south where there were still forests, came up with a plan designed not only to stabilise the dunes, but also to provide mass employment during its initial implementation – which would take more than twenty years – with a smaller number of permanent jobs in the future. But the investment would have to pay in the long term: monoculture of radiata pine was chosen with a view to timber harvesting in thirty-year cycles. By the early 1960s, agreement was reached with Māori traditional owners and the Aupōuri Forest was conceived.

Engaged as I am in a very different one-person mission – to vegetate the Dune in diverse native plants – I read with fascination E. V. Sale's *Forest on Sand*, recounting this massive reclamation project. It was decided that native grasses on the fore-dunes – primarily spinifex and *pīngao* – were too difficult to propagate in sufficient numbers for mass planting and neither would provide adequate shelter for tree seedlings. Instead, a nursery was set up in Sweetwater near the almond-eyed lake, on the peaty ground of a worked out gumfield. It would raise all the plants needed for the project, beginning with marram grass; ironically, marram, like spinifex and *pīngao*, requires moving sand to flourish, but marram anchors itself with roots two or three metres deep.

During the winters, from June to September, thousands of marram clumps were planted by hand and machine (depending on terrain) by work teams of mostly women, and nitrogen was sprayed by helicopter to enhance growth. Instead of gum-diggers shacks, clusters of canvas huts now marked the seasonal presence of each marram-planting gang along the tombolo. And all year round, the Sweetwater nursery raised not only marram, but also lupins for the next phase and radiata pine seedlings for the future. Once marram was established on the dunes, the work teams planted blue and yellow lupins. They would take hold, finally growing to a couple of metres to shelter tree seedlings from the winds. Lupins self-seed readily and fix nitrogen from the air in their roots to improve soil fertility.

Five years into the project, the sand was stable enough for the bright green tufty pine seedlings, only a few inches tall, to take their chances on the dunes. In what must have been a nail-biting operation, a month after the pines were planted, the whole area was sprayed with a weak herbicide to slow down the lupins sufficiently to reduce competition for the seedlings. After four years, the pines had grown to about five metres and were pruned for the first time, the debris left on the ground to rot as I do with the weeds I hack down on the Dune.

Today, the forest extends for some fifty miles along the inner dune belt from south to north of the tombolo, covering almost thirty-one thousand hectares; planted laboriously by hand where machine access was not possible. Pride in the accomplishment is clear in E. V.

Sale's account of the peak planting year: 'In the winter of 1983, 2.3 million radiata were planted over some 15 square kilometres of consolidated sand in two months.' It was a major achievement generating local employment, community participation, and a productive forestry industry that supports also a local particle board factory.

In a few more years, these endless silent ranks of pruned and thinned pine trees will again be harvested and replaced with new seedlings in monotonous regularity. While welcoming the economic benefits, and the fact that the Sweetwater Nursery did raise some local plants, including *kauri*, I cannot help wishing that priorities had included substantial areas for the permanent re-establishment of native forest diversity.

When I return along the plantation path to the Dune, my gaze into the lake's eye is enriched by a better appreciation of her story and her memories. As I sit for a while on the veranda, watching the comings and goings of the many lives that the lake supports, I am more determined than ever to help the Dune sustain native woodland.

I cannot see the frogs from the veranda, but their raucous choral renderings accompany hot afternoons and sultry evenings. Black swans with three or four cygnets in tow, mallard and paradise ducks, and Caspian terns are regular seasonal visitors, as are Canada geese. Stopping whatever I am working on to watch them delightfully interrupts my days – an occupational hazard for anyone attempting to write about nature. A few times, my vigilance has been rewarded by the excitement of seeing rare dabchicks fidgeting on the surface of shallower water near the shore. They tend to blend in among the lake-margin grasses and sedges with their understated plumage in fifty shades of grey, relieved only by a tan blush on neck and breast. And when I finally spot them, they dive for food and disappear. *Pūkeko*, though, are always somewhere plodging through the muddy lake edges to feed, their young ones skittering around them. *Pūkeko* nest in small groups, the whole community sharing the task of feeding and protecting the young.

Often, shortly after dawn, three or four *waka-ama* glide silently into view from behind a screen of trees, leaving a faint wake of silvery threads. I hear their urging chant when their outriggers become visible as they circumnavigate the lake, their crews practising this most ancient skill that brought their ancestors to these lands. A magical moment when centuries coalesce into the present.

Other human visitors are less benign. One small section of the shore is a grass flat accessible from the road for people who want to picnic, swim, or launch a dinghy from where the water laps a narrow strip of sand. A certain breed of fishermen and off-road enthusiasts make a habit of pulling in from the road and driving their trucks and trailers into the water to wash off the mud and salt accumulated from elsewhere. They contaminate the lake with invasive organisms from other sites, but the lake takes its own revenge. The water is rich in iron: they might as well spray their vehicles with liquid rust.

CHAPTER 5

DUNE IN SPRING AND SUMMER

Each spring on the Dune releases a fresh sense of urgency. Regular migrants and existing residents prepare nests for a coming generation. Swallows, sparrows, thrushes, white-eyes, fantails and tiny grey warblers swoop passed me trailing ambitious cargoes from their beaks: clumps of moss, bunches of dry grass, lengths of twine, even tangles of my hair brushed out some morning and blown into the bushes. The Dune has long since ceased to be silent. Unique canticles of birds, frogs, and insects mark the terce, nones and vespers of their days with renewed vigour.

I hear the tchi-tchi-tchi-tchi of the sacred kingfisher, the *kōtare,* all year round, but now it bears an added sharpness, a warning-off, as it flits between favourite perches overlooking a new nest-burrow in the bank alongside the drive. These tough, determined little birds excavate their burrows by flying into the bank over and over again, punching out a hole with their strong beaks. *Kōtare* are fiercely territorial. One morning I was watching one harassing another *kōtare* who was trespassing on his branch by rushing at him and flitting away without much effect, when he suddenly grabbed the interloper's tail feathers in his beak and swung on them from below. That worked. And everywhere I go, I am accompanied by a fantail, *pīwakawaka*, its song as elusive as itself: its incessant twittery verses so high in pitch they are barely audible to human ears. No wonder it is called the gossip of the woodland. No such problem with the sudden, sore-throated alarm screech of a pheasant and the deep craaaw of a heron passing on its way to the lake in the morning, or returning to roost before the sun is finally under the duvet.

The gleaming green-black, shot-silk back of the *tūī*, with its short lacy white shawl and distinctive white bobbles quivering at its throat, is seen more often at the birdbath in late spring and summer, swooping in fast and low from between the trees. It is fastidious, spending much longer bathing than other birds who have to wait their turn in the bushes. The *tūī's* mutterings and chortles and brief, squeaky-gate meditations wake me first in the mornings, and often accompany me unseen from some high tree branch while I work below. They are tree planters par excellence: first, pollinating flowers while they sip nectar from flax, *pūriri* and other flowering shrubs and trees, then eating the fruits and scattering the seed far and wide within a ten-kilometre feeding range. *Tūi's* distinctive flight is almost impossible to capture in a camera. With the force of only a couple of wing beats, their stream-lined bodies dive through the air like torpedoes, a long slightly curved beak aiming at a seemingly impenetrable bush, they shoot through and disappear into the foliage, only to reappear at the birdbath.

The real harbinger of spring, though, is the shining cuckoo, *pipiwharauroa*, named for its bronzed back shot through with green iridescence like a polished ancient artefact. The dark horizontal stripes on its throat and chest recall the suit of a jailbird; indeed, they have some anti-social instincts. The female lays one egg at a time in the nests of other birds, principally grey warblers, and flies off unheeding. Worse, their eggs incubate more quickly than those of their unsuspecting host, and when a shining cuckoo chick hatches, it tips the grey warbler's eggs out of the nest. Nature's drive is for survival.

Considering that shining cuckoo are no larger than a sparrow – though twice the size of their overworked foster parents – their voice soars above the forest choir in a clear, sustained soprano, almost a whistle, rising to a higher pitch as if to ask the question 'are you ready for spring?' This may be followed by a softer tone running down the scale, as if rewinding for the main aria. Contributors to the letters column of the local newspaper vie with each other to be the first to hear it in September or October.

If a wet spring and early summer sun have ripened the

grass, my neighbouring farmer cuts hay. Mesmerised, I watch his tractor-mounted mower laying down lines of cut grass in an artistic spiral around each steeply sloping field. And I am not the only watcher. Birds glean their share of hay for the foundations of their new nests. Initially, the golden strands are a give-away of nest locations but soon weather to biscuit-grey and blend invisibly into tree foliage, especially the tawny-green of tea tree.

The same swell of energy sends sap surging through stems erect, alert to their responsibility to make the most of this brief season of plenitude. But caution is necessary too. Trees and shrubs may appear to hesitate for years above ground, but their effort is focused on spreading down deep roots for their future. They are long-term strategists. Trees encouraged to grow too fast may not maintain their spring flush of tender growth during the dry season; the slow growers establish more securely and live longer – countless decades beyond the meagre span of our own impatient lives.

Some tree species have evolved as naturally fast growers with a short lifespan. The big-soft-floppy-leaved *whau* seems to shoot up but lives for only about ten years. Fast-growing trees leave a lot of air spaces between their woody cells, making the timber very light; *whau* is as light and buoyant as balsa wood. Perhaps in compensation for a short life, its seeds, encased in big fleshy burrs, germinate freely; the first *whau* I planted has already died a natural death and been replaced by three of its offspring. A third generation is springing up nearby.

It is human impatience that leads people to plant older, larger specimens of trees rather than smaller ones, although the younger sapling is likely to be more successfully established and even overtake the growth of a larger one. I knew this, but discovered it in practice after planting a young *kauri* that was less than a metre high. The following year, by chance, I was given a *kauri* sapling that was just over two metres. I planted it not far from the first, in the same conditions except that its survival required much more watering than its neighbour. Eight years later, the younger tree had caught up its older companion.

Such a clear comparison was possible only because the growing conditions were the same. The growth rate of young trees even of the same species varies enormously depending on what they have to cope with, and the more they have to struggle, the more vulnerable they are to the effects of insect attacks. We are all more resistant to disease and trauma when we enjoy the benefits of good food and a healthy lifestyle – an advantage sadly not accessible to everyone.

My learning curve as an accomplice is long and sometimes painful; the full results of my planting decisions not apparent for maybe eight or ten years. A one-metre *pūriri* sapling planted at the bottom of the south slope, where I had cut down an old banana clump and left it to rot, has grown three times the size of one planted at the same time and of the same size on top of the north slope. Inevitably I have made mistakes; there have been casualties and sad moments when attempts to sustain an ailing tree failed.

I had read advice about native tree culture and, in most cases, had selected planting sites with conditions within each species' natural range of tolerance. But to provide full larders for the bird population, I needed as much diversity as possible and I took risks. Some have paid off with careful nurturing in the early years; some have not. Both of those *pūriri* trees, though, are flowering and fruiting generously; the larger one, on damper, richer ground, is already surrounded by its own young. Eight others dotted about in various parts of the Dune are in different stages of maturity, the later planted ones have yet to flower.

Mānuka and *kānuka* also self-seed freely, their wispy grey-green seedlings pop up everywhere and I have to thin them out. Though they are two different species – *kānuka* grows to three times the height of *mānuka* which rarely reaches more than three metres, and its needle-leaves are softer to the touch than the stiff, tiny pointed leaves of *mānuka* – but since they look similar and their territory overlaps, most people refer to both as 'tea tree', the name given to *mānuka* by Captain Cook because his hosts gave him an infusion of its leaves as a tea substitute.

Tea tree were once extensive throughout the country; its remarkably wide tolerance, growing equally well in sand, bog, cold and heat, made it a natural pioneering tree, replacing other species unable to adapt as growing conditions changed or forest trees were felled. From their earliest days, Māori prized tea tree as a hard-wood timber for making spears and tools, as a hot-burning fuel for cooking fires, and for the healing qualities of its leaves and flowers. But whole swathes of tea tree woodlands were cleared by early European settlers to make way for cattle-grazing and crops – a continuing process which is now in decline thanks to another gift of tea tree.

Bees have always valued *mānuka* flowers for their sweet nectar, and the realisation in recent years that *mānuka* honey contains unique, powerful health qualities is encouraging both beekeeping and new plantings of *mānuka*. On the Dune, I thin out the mass of seedlings to create a sustainable supply of fuel. But of greatest value to me is tea tree's pioneering vigour to tackle and stabilise any ground, and its role as 'nurse' to other plants by providing light shade. Shade is often the key to a young sapling's survival, reducing evaporation of water from their tender leaves as well as from the soil.

Like so much in life, this benefit of nurse trees is not always trouble free. Tea tree are prone to infestations of 'sooty mould'. The trunk, limbs and leaves become encrusted with a slightly furry black coating, a fungus which gives off a sickly sweet odour caused by aphids feeding off the sap and producing what is euphemistically called 'honeydew'. Sticky honeydew and aphids drip onto plants beneath and mould spores quickly move in, and while an adult tea tree may be able to withstand the effects of fungus and aphids, new seedlings rarely can: the black coating on their leaves reduces the light they need for photosynthesis. I have treated new plants successfully with non-toxic Neem oil, but I am vigilant in checking on nurse trees and cutting back overhanging branches that suffer from sooty mould.

Another tough pioneering small tree that self-propagates freely from masses of little winged seeds is *akeake*, 'forever and ever', so named because the wood grain is tight and extremely strong and long-lasting. Older trees fling out thin bony arms in all directions with wild abandon, but the narrow main trunk is usually straight and was used traditionally to make spears and staffs – I use them myself to make stakes. With their thin, narrow lozenge-shaped leaves and open crowns they also make good nurse trees, but their eager proliferation creates another 'weeding' task to stop them crowding out other young trees. There is no lack of work to be done during the long-lit days that begin with first light at five-thirty in the morning and end with dusk around nine in the evening. But I am not the only creature that is frantically busy.

If the song of the shining cuckoo is the sign of spring, the herald of summer is the shrill rasping of massed cicadas, *kihikihi*, ear-piercing at close quarters. Whatever we may think of the din, it is a love song, a mating call which only the males make by contracting membranes, 'tymbals', on their abdomen. These high-pitched shrills are interspersed with rhythmical sharp clicks. The Māori name, *kihikihi*, describes the harsh sibilant sound of cicadas and is a metaphor for a noisy crowd: *Me kihi kei te waru* – 'Like cicadas in the eight month' (December in the Māori calendar). I was amused to discover that the English language of early settlers was also compared to the noise of cicadas – '*pakeha he kihikihi*'.

Each species of cicada has its own call to attract the

same species of female. And they can be forgiven for sounding so loud and desperate. Adult cicadas have only two or three weeks to live, having grown for several years underground as a nymph waiting for their brief conjugal moment.

After mating, the females lay their eggs in grooves they chew into plant stems. The tiny nymphs that hatch from them drop to the ground and burrow under the soil, tunnelling into plant roots to feed on the sap. They shed their outer casing, the exoskeleton, several times as they grow. When mature, and soil temperature tells them it is summer outside, they crawl up from their dark hiding place, settle on a tree trunk or wooden post, slough off their old coat for the last time, and stretch their wings ready for a short hectic life.

It was probably this apparent resurrection from the underworld of darkness that led to the cicada's adoption as a symbol of eternal life by the fifth-century Merovingian culture in what is now France. With elaborate optimism, the burial robe of the Frankish king, Childeric l, was emblazoned with gold cicadas. The tomb was discovered in the seventeenth century, confirmed as Childeric's by the signet ring and engraved portrait buried with him. Later generations misinterpreted the insect's identity, concluding that it was a bee; Napoleon Bonaparte, equally eager for immortality, adopted the golden 'bee' as the new symbol of the French Empire, displacing the ancient *fleur-de-lys*. In a cruel stroke of reality, in 1831, Childeric's ring and portrait were stolen from the National Library of France. Despite great efforts at the time, they have never been recovered.

In Māori tradition, it was the short life-span of cicadas that inspired the moral folk tale about the industrious ant who worked all summer to collect and store food for the winter, and the profligate cicada who refused to follow the ant's example, spending his days singing in the sunshine, until the food ran out as winter advanced and the cicada died.

The wisdom of nature is a universal inheritance. French poet and fabulist of the seventeenth century, Jean de la Fontaine, wrote a similar fable, '*La cigale et la fourmi*' ('The cicada and the ant') known to every child in France. And Fontaine's inspiration was Aesop's ancient tale of the ant and the grasshopper. In European stories, cicadas are often confused with crickets or grasshoppers because they both make a similar chirring sound for the same reasons, but in their case, they sing by rubbing the edges of their upper and lower wings together.

Clearly, the intricate web of connection exists not only underground, but above it: I was alerted to Childeric's story by an Irish medievalist, Dr Anne Marie D'arcy, and to Fontaine's fable by a French educationist, Marie-Hélène Thomas – we nourish each other's understanding across our shared planet.

Of the fifty species of cicada in the country, each adapted to their own ecological niche, ours in the sand country include the largest – and probably the loudest – the chorus cicada, whose vividly spangled body can be four centimetres long. I often find them on the timber walls of the cottage, motionless in their multicoloured glory, opening their crumpled wings after emerging from their buff-coloured cast left attached to the wall nearby.

My acquaintance with the eerily silent mantids, the praying mantis, *te whē*, is more intimate. They are housemates. Nearly every time I spend the day clambering among shrubs and trees on some task, I find a praying mantis has hitched a ride on my shoulder when I return to the house. And as doors and windows are left wide open during summer heat, others flit in and wander about whenever they fancy the underside of a coffee table or a shady crevice in a bookcase as an ideal place to lay their eggs. The female encases her eggs in a protective shell the colour and texture of a small oval glob of rough concrete, with a slightly raised seam along the mid-line.

When the young hatch, they obligingly eat fruit flies and mosquitoes, graduating to house flies and larger prey as they grow to adult size of around five centimetres – males are slightly smaller. At that stage, I escort them outside for a more adequate food supply. Usually, those who join me in the house are the native species, recognisable because they are pale green; those from elsewhere that I see are the colour of brown tree bark.

Watching their table manners, I think 'preying' mantis a more appropriate name. Their habit of posing, of seeming immobile, or of rocking gently to and fro while slowly turning their heads this way and that, is disarming. They are sizing up their prey. Their curious triangular heads have strong jaws in front and a large, exceptionally efficient eye on each of the other two corners. Once a mantis decides that what they are staring at is edible and within striking range, they are extremely agile. Lining the inside of those unctuously folded forelegs are rows of needle-sharp points like saw-teeth from which few victims can escape once gripped, especially when claws at the ends of other limbs are also brought into play. Even as the prey squirms ineffectually, whichever bit of its body is most quickly accessible is thrust into the mantis' mouth and voracious munching begins.

At least the mantis is not wasteful; everything is eaten – head, wings, legs, feet. And it is particular about hygiene: after the meal, the 'toothpick'. Tucked inside those grasping forelegs are tufts of fibres with which the mantis brushes its mouth and between the rows of saw-teeth to remove any remaining traces of food. The insatiable appetite of female mantids has given them a justifiable reputation for eating male partners after mating, but entomologists have observed that our canny native male has found a way of staying safely on her back: by swivelling the end of his body down to the underside of her abdomen, he completes the business without loss of his life.

As the season progresses, mid-summer sun arcs directly overhead; dead bracken rasps and crumbles under my boots, the air parched and papery. Sun's scorching stare so intense that blue sky fades to hot white. The very air is exhausted. Unless I can find a patch in shade, I can work outside only in early morning and late evening. While I am stooping, clipping, digging, raking, tiny flickering gossipy fantails hover around my every movement; to them I am a harmless lumbering animal, an unwitting beater driving insects from their coveys to be caught on the wing. In their company, I continue to clear the scrub a small section at a time ready for planting the following season.

Summer is an anxious time. It brings the stress of drought and risk of fire as both vegetation and sand dry out quickly despite my efforts to keep the ground well covered with mulch – debris from clearing, bracken, bought-in bark, whatever I can provide. Young trees strain to find the moisture they crave and must be watered. The fine roots of even semi-mature trees shrivel if they dry out, and although a wet winter may follow, they are unlikely to recover the root-loss quickly enough before the next summer and may die unexpectedly two or three years after a severe drought. During the last drought, the greatest losses were tree ferns which had grown unexpectedly from spores that must have lingered in the ground for years. Their moment of optimism was mistimed; they require huge quantities of water that I cannot provide.

The Dune and I share a single rain-water tank: all there will be of this precious life force until the rains return. Though we have occasional rain in summer, some years we have been without for six or eight weeks at a time while temperatures approach the early thirties. I have become an obsessive sky-watcher, searching for any signs of a shower. A frustrating exercise as, day after day, what I call the 'teasing clouds' hover over us: I can see the water in those dusky clouds, smell it, but no rain falls. When I go to the beach at low tide, and see a line of creamy curdled clouds along the horizon mimicking the white sea foam beneath them until the two are indistinguishable – sea in the sky and sky in the sea – it seems a perfect depiction of earth's water cycle. But its patterns are becoming increasingly unpredictable.

I ration my own water use while the trees are young and need it more than I do. As an exponent of the one-pan-one-bowl meal, I can limit washing-up to every second or third day. The restriction causes me no regret, though I have not yet sunk to the squalor of dispensing with the bowl and eating out of the pan. Skill in rapid showering was learned with bucket-showers while working in Papua New Guinea. For anyone unfamiliar with this device, here is my description from *Inside the Crocodile*: 'It was an upturned bucket with holes drilled into a rotatable plate at the bottom, dangling by a rope from the roof. Water was at a premium in the drier season and I learned the technique of the 'half-bucket shower': wet the skin, stop the water by turning the plate that blocked the holes, soap all over, start the water again and rinse while spinning rapidly on the spot. If trusted with a full bucket of water, it was a point of honour to leave as much as possible for the next person.' So few clothes are worn in summer that hand-washing is easy and the water is saved for plants or flushes the toilet. All of these small actions help, but effective water conservation must be planned for.

When the cottage was built I installed a grey-water system: a tank under the house which collects water from the shower and laundry sink for re-use on plants. And an additional small water tank beside the nursery strip is fed by run-off from the garage roof; it supplies the shade house and ranks of pots in trays on the ground. Town-dwellers may not realise that the availability of tank water depends on a reliable power supply to pump it from the tank to the house and to an outside tap. (In Papua New Guinea, it had to be pumped by hand. A laborious arm-aching exercise; there are few stronger incentives to conserve water use.) As power cuts are not unusual here, the nursery tank also has a tap at its base, so that I can draw water by gravity – an emergency supply for both the seedlings and myself.

One way or another, newly planted saplings have priority when water is scarce. If I can keep them strong until their roots are down far enough, in a few years they will find and conserve their own water. Eventually, they will form fungal partnerships below ground to assist them, but if, after two or three years of watering, they do not thrive, they probably never will and it is pointless trying to maintain them artificially unless there is some special reason for doing so. The loss of any tree is sad. And as seasonal temperatures increase with climate change, others who cannot cope will die, but the most robust and adaptable will continue to thrive – a compelling reason for diversity of plants and planting sites.

Although my purpose is to establish native woodland on the Dune, I planted a few well-behaved camellias on the south-facing slope, and indulged in a small area of other exotics on the east side, on top of the Dune close to the cottage. In this small circular garden, tropical *Vireya rhododendrons* and azaleas are arranged around a central birdbath and shaded by encircling native trees. A surrounding, simple wooden pergola supports a couple of rambling roses when scavenging possums leave enough buds uneaten, and there is a seat to rest. I persevere with these few roses, despite their regular ravishment, because possums seem to prefer their tender red shoots to anything else; the *pūriri* tree which now partially overhangs the circular garden has never shown any possum damage. Beside the *pūriri* is an Australian banksia that I have allowed to grow because it produces nectar-rich brush-like flower heads all year round. *Tūī* love these so much as a food source that successive pairs have inhabited the tree for years; for them it must be like living over a deli with a swimming pool in the courtyard.

This little oasis around the birdbath is a quiet memorial to the people I have lost. From my study, I see the almond-eyed lake through one window, and the round garden through the other and it offers endless entertainment.

On hot days, the birds are queuing up in the bushes for a bath. Each has its own routine. The kingfisher dives straight from a tree branch, scoots through the water and out the other side a couple of times before standing on the edge to take brief furtive dips. Perhaps the dive is to test the water, or to stake his turn, but I suspect it is for sheer joy. *Tūī* takes bathing far more seriously.

He plunges and wriggles a dozen times and emerges on the rim dripping and bedraggled, the fluffy white pom-poms at this throat reduced to dripping strings. Little white-eyes and fantails generally favour the security of communal bathing. Always watchful, they dip and flutter rapidly, darting back and forth into the bushes.

Visiting Australian parrots, Eastern rosella, are far more indulgent in the bath. Flashing their bright red, green, yellow and iridescent blue plumage they duck under the water, splashing around with abandon like cavorting clowns and half empty the bath before they finally give someone else a turn. In summer heat, birds are driven half crazy by mites. Male blackbirds seem to suffer especially and bathe often, ducking repeatedly until they are thoroughly wet, and employing impossible-seeming contortions to scratch the back of their head with their feet, revealing patches of bare skin. They rest for a while on the rim of the bath, dishevelled, bodies hunched to splay the feathers out, and then begin the whole process again. It makes me feel itchy to watch them; and a relief to see them complete their grooming and pause, sleek and comfortable once again, before flying off.

In between bath times there are other antics to watch. *Vireya*, tropical Rhododendron which often grow as epiphytes in their natural montane-forest habitats, thrive where their roots enjoy rapid drainage yet have access to air and moisture. As the round garden is one of the driest spots on the Dune, it has to be watered during dry periods, and I keep the ground covered in a thick layer of bark mulch. Through this, blackbirds, especially the females —mother blackbirds who forage ceaselessly – dig furiously to expose worms and bugs; the drier it becomes the deeper and more frantically they work. They dig with their feet like chickens, flinging bits of bark over their shoulders with their beaks. When they expose plant roots, I cover them with more mulch until the blackbird's next foraging session throws it around again. Our game of hide and seek goes on all summer, nurturing plants, birds, and writer. It is a wonder I find time to write at all.

A more important use for the circular pergola in the round garden was to plant a native vine, a liana, of which only one specimen still exists in the wild. A single plant of *Tecomanthe speciosa* was found by scientists in 1945 on Three Kings Islands in a spot inaccessible to the goats which had ravaged the rest. Although other kinds of *Tecomanthe* inhabit tropical areas of Asia and the Pacific, this solitary plant appears to be the only survivor of its species.

Botanists visited Three Kings Islands to take cuttings of the plant; a decade later the cuttings had grown to produce their own seed, and horticulturists germinated the seeds, making plants available to gardeners. I did not expect to be swinging from the liana but I wanted to grow it in the round garden if I could. As it turned out, I enjoyed only one season of its gorgeous cream, waxy trumpet flowers before it died back. The site was probably too dry, chosen out of a selfish desire to watch it grow nearby; one I planted at the base of the south slope shot straight up the trunk of a tree – if it is flowering, at least the birds will take pleasure from the nectar.

I left the half rotted stump of the liana in the ground to complete its decay. I was sure it was dead. But nature's default position is renewal of life. Several years later, the vine sent out two new stems that have now reached the crossbeam of the pergola and I hold my breath that it will continue and produce flowers again. *Tecomanthe* flowers grow in a tight cluster straight out of the stem and are much larger than most native blooms.

Contrary to how it may appear, I am not a 'keen gardener'. I am simply a tree planter. I inherited no family traditions of flower beds and vegetable patches. In the family album were photographs of a benevolent but stiff-looking gentlemen leaning on a sundial in a rose garden who was, I was told, my maternal grandfather; an architect, he had died and the house sold long before I was even thought of. My paternal grandfather, a retired parson in the Isle of Man when I knew him, lived with my grandmother and aunt in a semi-detached house with only a square of lawn at the back, a few flowering bushes – in my mind's eye I see golden sprays of forsythia – and a large wooden shed full of bric-a-brac – a cave of amazing treasure to a child. All of this was the accumulation of years, but my parents moved a lot. We lacked the stability and continuity to establish gardens even had there been the wish. At the back of our various farm cottages rough grass and a seedy blackcurrant bush or two struggled in a small barren wilderness given over to dogs and chicken pens. Nothing dared raise its head above the soil.

My schoolgirl memories are not of the rosy, carefree

kind. Moving as we did so often from one farm to another, one area to another, wherever there was work, I was perpetually the 'new girl'. I was dressed more shabbily than most pupils in these small rural schools, but the real trigger for the endless bullying I endured was every word I spoke. Staying nowhere long enough to absorb the local dialect, I had only to open my mouth to be revealed as an alien. The fear of 'difference', which seems in so many people to continue into their adult life, may have had survival value at some early point in our evolution, but today, our tribe is all of humanity; diversity is the key to our future existence, as it is for the workings of nature.

Seasonal cycles were already a familiar pleasure to me: I was kept out of school to help thin 'neeps' – turnips – in spring, and to harvest hay in autumn. But my interest in a garden was entirely independent. My first efforts blossomed when I was nine or ten years old, though it was more of a cemetery than a garden. We were living in the rural depths of Sussex, England, where my father was dairyman and general farm worker for a small estate in the neighbourhood. Our tied farm cottage was just within the three-mile limit beyond which council assistance was given for transport, so I had a long walk to school each day.

As I meandered unwillingly to the drudgery of lessons, I would come across dead birds, squashed frogs, and hedgehogs that failed to reach the other side of the road. If I was on my way to school, I hid them in the hedge until my return when I carried them carefully home for burial. My little cemetery, a strip along the base of the cottage wall, grew quite lush with dandelions, nasturtiums, marigolds and daisies. At that young age I did not know why the flowers grew so well, how they were nurtured from the creatures decaying beneath them. The purpose was simply to resolve my sadness at the loss of life, and mark their place with something bright and pretty. Whether I was aware of it or not, my cemetery garden provided the first faint glimmer of nature's cycle of death and renewal. And I was against untimely death. I never cut my flowers to bring indoors, but left them to live out their natural life-span. When we were each given a daffodil in nature study class, and told to cut it in half to see what was inside, I refused to cut mine. The teacher took it away and sent me to stand in the corridor.

It was at this period of my life that I first became enthralled by trees. There was an ancient forest beyond our wilderness of a back garden, protected by a high deer fence. The green mysteries and murmurings of these old trees were a fascination to me, and the fact that they were fenced off and forbidden was a challenge that spurred my regular trespass. Trying not to tread on mosses and tiny plants, I would walk up to these gnarled giants and lean against their trunks, tracing the wrinkles and contours of their bark with my fingers. Looking up into the canopy through the elfin light that made anything seem possible, I imagined that the trees spoke to each other. I longed to know what stories they told. In a troubled childhood it was my secret place of quiet joy.

But I got caught. Not by the gamekeeper but by my

own clumsiness. As I was climbing down one afternoon, the inner part of my arm snagged on the barbed-wire strung along the top of the deer fence. I kept very still because my weight was supported only by a dent in the fence that my feet rested on precariously, and by the fingers of my other arm, already turning white with their desperate grip of the thin wire mesh. Fortunately, a neighbour heard my call for help and lifted me up carefully to release my arm from the barbs. I still have the small scar, two raised white puncture marks where the points dug in and began to tear; it reminds me occasionally of the risks we take to achieve what we value.

Keen gardeners tend to raise vegetables and fruit for the table, and flowers for display, the bolder and more vivid the better. Many plant annuals along borders and re-design their flower beds every few years. Growing forest trees requires a different sort of ambition and much more patience. Apart from the longer time-scale – most of us will never see the trees we plant reach full maturity – we have less control: the trees are the dominant partner. And with a few exceptions, woodland and forest trees are not grown to display their flowers.

The flowers of most of our native trees in New Zealand are small and often white or pale green: they reward getting up close and personal. The flower buds of *akeake* are little bigger than a pin head, yet they open into intricate, stubby-petalled whitish flowers that bees can access; *ngaio's* tiny white flowers are prettily stippled with red dots; and though *pūriri*, *karo* and other pittosporums have red bell-like flowers ranging in tone from crimson to maroon, they too are extremely small, no more than a centimetre across. The numerous species of coprosma and corokia shrubs generally bear even smaller yellow or green flowers, but parade their wares more vividly with masses of orange, blood-red, yellow, and magenta berries – an excellent source of bird food.

Though in ever so many shades, perpetual evergreen can occasionally feel monotonous and one yearns for more dramatic colour. In the spring, I am always grateful for the flaming funnels of flax flowers, and the splendid butter-cup yellow pendants of sophora, *kōwhai*, massed like a golden crown with flowers that occasionally come out before the leaves (one of our few sometimes-deciduous trees). Though less vivid in colour, the frothy cream flower clusters of golden *tainui*, *kumarahou*, are a welcome early sign of spring's awakening. A tough pioneering shrub with thick, wrinkled dark-green leaves, *kumarahou* live only for a few years but self-seed confidently in any open ground. The leaves create lather when rubbed in wet hands, a feature that earned it the nick-name, 'gum-diggers soap'. Purple stars of solanum, *poroporo* (a relative of the potato), brightened the north-facing slope for a while, but this spindly, fast-growing pioneer biennial made only a fleeting appearance and disappeared from the Dune as vegetation cover thickened. Another leggy pioneer plant, native hibiscus, *puarangi*, continues to colonise any sunny spaces with a single flower atop peculiarly hairy stems, its fragile buff-white petals delicately etched inside with maroon.

Flax, *harakeke*, is among the most generous of plants. In addition to their uplifting flamboyant spring colour, and their strong, strap-like leaves indispensable to weavers, they accumulate in the base of their deep narrow funnels the sweetest nectar. Nectar is an important part of *tūī* diet; their long, slim, slightly downward curving beaks are an adaptation to this food source in a range of flowers. But they face competition: black birds, starlings, and mynah birds, though less well adapted, thrust their sharp straight beaks into the flowers whenever they can evade the assertive *tūī*. Worse, the clumsy rosella, not content that their short hooked beaks give them an advantage in accessing seeds, nuts and fruit, lust after nectar as well. They cannot push their fat beaks into the narrow funnels of flax flowers; instead, they grab them with their feet and chew at their base to suck out the nectar, leaving the flowers too damaged to accumulate more nectar later in the day. So far, I have not seen magpies, the other exotic hooligans of the forest, ravage the flax flowers and hope they stay away from them.

Looking out of the study windows invariably results in delightful diversions when I am supposed to be writing. The other day, three young welcome swallows were balancing, a little precariously, on a branch of a small tree in the dappled shade of its feathery leaves. At intervals, they made brief fluttery flights, returning almost immediately to their branch. One of them suddenly thrust its head forward and stretched open its bright yellow beak wider than seemed possible, revealing an eager pink throat: it had seen a parent approaching

View from the top of the Dune, "Sky and lake have no secrets from each other."

"All over this landscape, ancient dunes nudge and over-ride each other in arrested motion."

Early years, cutting paths and steps.

North-facing slope in 2020.

Part of south slope after 8 years; below, after 20 years.

Coprosma

Kawakawa

Kowhai

Manuka

Juvenile kotare demanding food.

Welcome swallow feeding a fledgling

The tree house (the green sail was torn down in a gale).

*Te Oneroa-a-Tōhē ('the Long Beach of Tōhē),
or Ninety Mile Beach.*

Pohutukawa

Long tresses of rimu

Totara chief of the forest

Puriri

The first-planted kauri tree

Flowers of Rewarewa tree, NZ honeysuckle

Poor Knights Lily, toothbrush plant

Piwakawaka (Fantail); Kotare (Sacred Kingfisher)

Matuku moana (white-faced heron)

Tui in the dawn light, and sleek after a bath

Acrobatic Tauhou (white-eye or wax-eye)

Winter sunrise over the lake

with food. Hovering on the wing, the parent thrust the dragonfly from her beak into the waiting throat and darted off for more.

The view through the kitchen window is equally diverting and explains the aroma of burnt toast lingering through the house most mornings. From the sink, I watch *kōtare*, the kingfishers, perch on a favourite branch of a casuarina tree to catch the first warmth of sunrise, and on a nearby tea tree branch in the evening, facing the setting sun. Both trees overlook the steep bank alongside the drive into which each new generation of *kōtare* punches out their nesting burrows, and it is from these favourite branches that their fledglings make their first faltering flights. They, too, demand food from harassed-looking parents but are fed differently: bugs and grubs are passed from the parent's long beak to the fledgling's beak – they must learn to keep hold of the food before tipping it back into their own throats. As whales swim through shoals of tiny fish with their mouths open to scoop them up, swallows flit back and forth through the air scooping up insects in their short open beaks.

The season's surprises lighten the long days of watering, weeding and mulching. And if I can muster enough energy after my summer chores are done, I go down to the beach and the delicious coolness of a sea breeze. Though neither fisher nor surfer, I consult the anglers' tide charts because the coincidence of high tide and sunset is potentially a moment of high drama in the beach's long, enthralling story.

CHAPTER 6

BEACH

We have arrived at the beginning of the big story within which mine is but a single grain of sand. At the 'old sea-salt of a great-great-grandfather', an ancestor not only of the Dune, the lake and the swamp, but also of the whole sandspit that is the Aupōuri tombolo: the turbulent sea – the domain of Tangaroa, the Māori sea god.

The sea that gave birth to the dunes brought the first human inhabitants from across the Pacific in their *waka*; the early explorers, traders and European settlers in sailing ships like winged seeds; and later, settlers in steam ships.

I sit on a sand dune watching the western horizon. Today, the waves are patient, a gently cascading sequence of blue-green bolts of satin edged with white lace, unrolling with persuasive persistence. Only as they greet the shore do they break up into bustling exploring eddies whispering to the sand the gossip of where they have been and what they have brought back. Gifts they leave on the shore: a few shells, necklaces of delicate seaweeds, and billions more tiny crystals of quartz to join those on the beach. Mineral stains in wet sand embroider intricate sepia patterns, unique designs created by each ebbing tide in infinite variety – until the sun dries them, restoring the canvas to soft pale crystalline sand ready for the ingenuity of the next advancing tide.

On stormy nights the waves rear up, roaring at each other through the darkness, jostling to be the first to the finishing line, their wind-whipped curdling crests beating down the shore like demented ghosts spattering foam as they fume at the sand. At high tide they hew chunks from the dunes, leaving them flat faced and scarred. They will dry in time, wind and gravity smoothing their contours again. In this mood, waves leave behind them heavier cargos, trees with severed roots sticking up in futile gestures at the sky, old tyres, ropes, bits broken off wrecked boats, dead birds, and huge tangles of seaweed wrenched from the seabed and dragged up to the beach.

These are the daily rituals of erosion and deposition; the work of wind, rain and wave, the planet's perpetual cycle of destruction and creation. And such the irascibility of the weather god, Tāwhirimātea, the brother of Tāne, so angered by the separation of his parents, Papatūānuku and Ranginui, that he left his siblings to join his father in the sky and vent his rage over land

and sea. His storm surges are orchestrated by shrieking wind and raging thunder hammering torrential rain out of dark anvil clouds. Stunted *pōhutukawa* trees cowering behind the fore dunes, backs bent to the wind, give testimony to Tāwhirimātea's frequent bad temper.

From my vantage point, looking north, I see a long straight sweep of dunes, beach and sea merging with the sky into a far distant haze towards Cape Reinga. To the south, a similar scene, though the land is curved slightly outward to end in a raised headland at Tauroa point, volcanic remains on what was once the end of North Island, before the sandspit joined it to the isolated rocky islands strung out further north. Had I sat here about a hundred-thousand years ago, the view would have been much the same, but I would have been sitting several kilometres inland as the tombolo was then newly formed and much narrower.

It all began with the other ancestors, the disruptive volcanic side of the family. The full story of the whole of North Island is told by Bruce Hayward in *Out of the Ocean into the Fire,* from which we can trace the 'genealogy' of the tombolo.

A string of isolated, rocky islands remained where volcanoes exploded during the chaotic eons when Zealandia broke away from Gondwana. Zealandia was deeply submerged several times, thrust up and submerged again by seismic seizures, while widespread volcanic eruptions continued building mountains and ridges. But between three and four million years ago, the Pacific Plate under the ocean rammed and overrode the northern part of Zealandia, setting off a further round of volcanic and seismic activity and raising the continental shelf, leaving the line of rocky islands in the far north standing in shallow water instead of deep ocean.

From that time, as rain and wind eroded the volcanic landscape of central North Island, rivers washed eroded particles into the sea to west and east, and this sediment was carried north by prevailing sea currents. Sand and debris accumulated along the shallow coastlines. Snagged on rocks and built up in bays and inlets, it began to form coastal dunes. In recent research, geologists have found exposed remnants of ancient cemented dunes attached to rock outcrops that were the eastern edges of those isolated rocky islands before the tombolo was built: most notably at Cape Reinga, Houhora, and Cape Karikari.

By a million years ago, more dunes had joined these pioneers, forming a not-quite-continuous band like the curved rib of a coat-hanger from Tauroa Point in the south to Cape Reinga in the north; east-facing dunes were likely built up from sediments washed from the volcanic fields of central North Island by rivers flowing into the Bay of Plenty, especially by the Waikato River which, at that time, flowed east.

Extending this early dune belt to form the present tombolo was an extremely slow process. It has been estimated that mud and sand carried by the sea travelled north at the rate of about two kilometres per century. Deposited on the shallow sea bed, it formed the sand-store from which the sea threw sand upon the shore. But that is only the start. There is the sea's tussle of give and take: when sea levels were low, more sand was left on the beach to form dunes, but during storm surges and periods of higher sea levels, waves snatched back the sand. This rhythm of changing sea levels balances the volume of sand on the sea-bed with that on the shore. When the sand-store is overfull, excess sand is thrown onto the beach; when it is too empty, sand is scraped back from fore dunes and beach.

Such changes in sea level occurred with each passing ice age because ice traps the planet's water and sea levels fall; when the ice melts – as they are doing rapidly now in our climate crisis – water is released and sea levels rise. (Though we tend to think only of the most recent Ice Age, regular cycles of 'ice ages' and warming have occurred for most of the planet's four billion years of existence; only the present rate of man-made heating is unprecedented.) But two traumatic events later speeded up the accumulation of sand and filled out the tombolo on its western flank.

Taranaki, on North Island's west coast, has been a centre of volcanic activity for over two million years, where multiple cones and lava fields were worn down and replaced by successors. The present Maunga Taranaki (previously known as Mount Egmont) began erupting a hundred-and-thirty thousand years ago; eruptions that recurred roughly every five-hundred years, producing masses of debris that was gradually washed up the west coast to the Far North.

A further boost to the sand supply came from Taupo volcano. Though its central crater or caldera has long since collapsed and filled with water, Taupo volcano has been regularly and aggressively active for the last three-hundred-thousand years. And although the best known eruption took place a mere eighteen-hundred years ago (in AD232) when a plume from the volcano's central vent shot fifty kilometres into the air, a much earlier eruption significantly affected the Aupōuri tombolo.

When the Oruanui eruption burst out of Taupo volcano twenty-five thousand years ago, it spewed so much debris that it blocked the Waikato valley. The Waikato River was diverted to flow west and north (its present course), where it carried additional volcanic sediments to the west coast. Since then, the width of the tombolo doubled, aided greatly by lower sea levels. Today, for most of its hundred-kilometre length, the Aupōuri Peninsula is little more than ten kilometres wide.

While I have been sitting here on a sand dune overlooking the beach, musing on the wonders of nature that created this strip of land, a playful breeze has thrown soft sand over my feet. And I marvel at the tiny particles of ancient volcanoes caught between my toes. It seems equally wonderful to me that modern scientists can analyse the minerals in these sand grains and estimate not only their age, but also the likely volcano that gave birth to them as lava and ash before they solidified and were worn down to a single grain.

In this intriguing story, the sea is more than merely a means of transport and storage of migrating sediments. What the rivers throw into it – flakes of rock, ash, volcanic sediments, alluvial mud – the sea tumbles, polishes, sifts and transforms. Heavier particles like iron-bearing sands are dropped first; the light white quartz is carried furthest; and some material is worn away entirely. Very little black, iron sand reaches the Far North, only a faint trace to tint the elaborate embroideries of receding waves.

The whole enchanted process continues. The beach in front of me, the fore dunes alongside me, and the rolling overlapping sandhills behind me have all been washed up and blown forward over the last eight thousand years. We inhabit a living, breathing landscape with a heartbeat. Further inland, older dunes have been fixed in position by human interventions of pine plantations and pastures, but at the beach, the tussle between Tangaroa's moods of give and take continues. Studies suggest that sea levels here rose by roughly a third of a metre over the last century; a rate that will increase with the current speed of ice-melt resulting in greater coastal erosion.

But there is more than one way to tell a good story. Māori mythology provides a poetic version of this land's origins through the actions of Māui. Though Māui's parents were lesser gods and Māui possesses supernatural strength, he is more of a cultural hero than a god. While his parents lived in the land of spirits, Māui lived with his adoptive family in their Polynesian homeland, the island of Hawaiki.

Young Māui longs to join his four older brothers on their fishing expeditions. They always refuse him because he is known as a mischievous trickster and they are secretly a little afraid of him. But Māui is determined to be a champion fisherman. He persuades his divine ancestress, Murirangawhenua, to lend him her jaw bone to carve into a beautiful fishhook, and learns from her a powerful *karakia* or ritual chant to use with it.

The night before his brothers' next fishing trip, Māui hides in their *waka*, their canoe, his special fishhook tied to a flax rope concealed beneath his cloak. In the morning, once his brothers have paddled the *waka* well away from the island, Māui reveals his presence with a cheeky greeting. Angered at being tricked, his brothers start to turn the boat to take him back to the shore. But he convinces them that he will be useful to bail out the boat and they let him stay. When they arrive at their usual fishing ground, Māui persuades them to go further out to sea. Each time they prepare to anchor and fish, Māui urges them to go further and further, assuring them that he knows a potent *karakia* that will attract the fish.

Eventually, the *waka* reaches the wide ocean beyond the sight of land, way beyond the distance anyone has been before. And when the brothers throw out their hooks and lines, they catch whole shoals of fish which soon fill the boat. As they prepare to return home well satisfied, Māui begs them to wait and let him fish too.

They do not believe he has a fishhook. When he shows them his hook and line they scoff and refuse to give him any of their bait. Undaunted, Māui punches his nose to make it bleed, smears his blood over the hook, and casts his line far over the sea.

The fishhook sinks deeper and deeper into the water until it reaches the ocean floor. There, the line grows taut and Māui uses all his strength to hold it as the sea suddenly rears up into huge waves roaring and rolling around them. His brothers fear for their safety and urge him to cut the line, but Māui doubles his efforts to draw it in, shouting Murirangawhenua's *karakia* into the turbulence with all the force of his lungs.

Māui brings the fish to the surface and sees that it is land, Papa-tu-a-nuku (literally, 'a flat land spread wide'). It is North Island, the tail-fin of the fish ending in the two points of Cape Reinga and North Cape.

There is much more to this myth – the brothers greedily hacking at the great fish (cutting the mountains and ridges of the landscape) and quarrelling over its distribution, while the canoe becomes the foundation of South Island – but it bears a core truth of the land's uplift from the ocean bed amid seismic chaos. Nineteenth-century scholar, Francis Dart Fenton, whose account I have drawn upon, describes the legend of Māui and the great fish as widely known throughout the Pacific, an ancient story long before Polynesians reached Aotearoa (New

Zealand), and suggests its origin from earlier migrations of Polynesian mariners in their gradual discovery and peopling of the Pacific Islands. This seems likely, including the inevitable quarrels about distribution and ownership of discovered lands.

To me, a special significance of the story is that Māui is not a god. He is a hero, albeit with super-human powers. It would have been so easy for the gods to have created the land, but human agency in this myth suggests not only Pacific history of exploration and discovery, but also a human responsibility for the land: the potential to ruin it and the necessity to care for it. Inevitably, land was also worth fighting for. The tombolo, the dunes and lakes behind it, tell many stories of early conflicts between neighbouring peoples, but it is a poignant personal legend that gave the beach its name: Te Oneroa-a-Tōhē – the Long Beach of Tōhē.

Tōhē, chief of the Ngāti Kahu people, lived in a village at the very top of the Peninsula, in a bay between the tail fins of the great fish. An old man, Tōhē yearned to see his daughter before he died. Many years before, Rāninikura had married into a family near what is now Dargaville some three-hundred kilometres south. Brushing aside the concerns of his people – that he was too old; it was too far – Tōhē walked around the bay and over the hills to the west coast and began his long journey south along the beach. For food and water, the sands yielded *toheroa*, a succulent clam; the sea offered abundant fish; the skies teemed with birds; and many freshwater streams flowed out to the coast. At night, Tōhē sheltered among the dunes, gathered wood for his fire, and bathed in dune lakes. Along the way, he named the places and natural features he passed.

As the old man began to tire, his desire to see Rāninikura urged him on; way beyond the long beach and as far again down the coast of Northland to Maunganui Bluff. He was within thirty kilometres of his daughter's village, but their reunion was not to happen in this life. Tōhē's body was worn out and his spirit departed.

Before he left his people, Tōhē had instructed them to ensure his spirit returned if he died on the way. And that is why the bay between the tail fins of the great fish is called Kapowairua (Spirits Bay). An aged *pōhutukawa* tree clings to the rocky headland of Te Rerenga Wairua ('leaping place of spirits'), and from its roots the spirits of the dead take their final leap to return to their origins in Hawaiki. The souls of the departed follow the sun's path dipping below the western horizon, as did those of my Celtic ancestors.

Like ancient sand grains shifting in wind and sea, past and present, myth and fact, intertwine to enrich our understanding of landscape: the long beach is part of Te Ara Wairua, the 'Spirits Way', en route to Te Rerenga Wairua, the eastern tail fin of the Māui's great fish, and the remains of one of the isolated volcanic islands from eons past that were joined together by the migrating sands of the tombolo.

Though there are far fewer birds along the coast now than in Tōhē's time, they, too, are characters in this marvellous drama. Bird migrations were among navigational aids used by Polynesian mariners; their flight path would lead to land. The bar-tailed godwit, *kuaka*, migrates across the Pacific Ocean from its breeding grounds in Alaska to spend summers in New Zealand, and was likely one of the species followed by *waka* as the birds approached land in September each year.

The pale brown and grey speckled *kuaka* are a common sight in the warm waters of Northland, and on dune fringes and wetlands. They also visit the almond-eyed lake, wading on long legs, their straight spear-like beaks rummaging around in soft mud. In March, those that are ready to breed – four year olds, the males' breast feathers now a pinkish blush ready for courting – assemble in full voice around Te Rerenga Wairua to begin the long return journey to Alaska. Their high-pitched chivvying call, 'awik-awik … wiki-wiki-wiki', seems to urge fellow travellers to prepare themselves. This time, their route will be via staging posts along the western shores of the Pacific. In a poetic closing of the circle, it is said that *kotuku*, the white heron, takes the spirits of the dead along the beach and across to Te Rerenga Wairua, and *kuaka* accompany them into the Pacific for the start of their journey to the west.

The presence of other sea and land birds, seasonal migrants who breed here, reward patient walks along the beach: gannets, shearwaters, terns, petrels, welcome swallows, and occasionally penguins who nest among the dunes. Of these, I see most often the whale-birds, a petrel, their effortless wheeling and diving powered by warm air currents. As they watch the stranding waves nibble at the sand, perhaps the birds are working up an appetite for their next meal. Terns frequently explore the lake, and welcome swallows soar and swoop over the Dune, hunting insects in flight, dive-bombing me on the veranda without compunction.

As it was for Tōhē, the long beach was always a thoroughfare and rich food source for Māori; a popular place for summer camps to gather seafood, to hunt birds and, later, to dig for *kauri* gum.

After the first British missionaries and settlers moved in to colonise Northland – from the early nineteenth century – they, too, saw potential in the long flat strands of sand. Old maps give several different names to the beach, including Sandy Neck, but local settlers called it 'Ninety Mile Beach'. Despite the fact that the beach is not quite sixty miles long, the name stuck. Why this is so occasionally tickles the curiosity of tourists. In response to a visitor's query some fifty years ago, the archivist at the Alexander Turnbull Library made a thorough search of historical sources but was unable to solve the mystery. And he found no evidence to support a popular explanation that an early French explorer had measured the beach in kilometres, later misquoted as miles. Although the beach does measure roughly ninety kilometres, there is more to naming than bald facts: 'Ninety-Mile' was thought by settlers to have a better ring to it.

Local newspaper reports of events on the beach flag the general development of the colony. Shipwreck Bay, at the southernmost part of the beach is named with good reason. Schooners, paddle steamers, and fully-rigged sailing ships have all perished in the vicinity. Perhaps the most memorable was the cargo ship *SS Ventnor*, sailing in 1902 from Wellington to Hong Kong with a freight of coal and the remains of some five-hundred Chinese miners who had been working in South Island gold fields. A Chinese charity had arranged for their exhumation from local cemeteries for transport back to China for traditional burial. The ship hit a reef, and later sank off Hokianga Heads. Many of the crew were saved in three of the ship's lifeboats, but the fourth was washed up, empty, on Ninety Mile Beach. Later, human bones in a canvas bag were found among flotsam at the base of a dune. Having been identified as part of *Ventnor's* cargo, they were repatriated to China.

Horseback was the principal means of travel across scrub-covered dunes and between isolated gum-fields and settlements, and horse racing had long been a popular local sport along stretches of the beach. But after the first horseless carriage was driven up to the Far North in 1906, and considering the rutted condition of the few tracks in the area where bullock carts and strings of packhorses held sway, it was not long before the beach became a roadway from one end of the peninsula to the other. By 1911, the Auckland Automobile Association was organising regular car race meetings over the sands, attracting fifty or more entrants from all over the country, and hailing Ninety Mile Beach as 'the speedway of the future'.

The beach's reputation as a place for touring – for those with money and leisure to do so – was enhanced by the visit of Sir Godfrey Fell, a senior British official in the colonial Far East administration. Sir Godfrey and his entourage drove the length of the beach in 1917, declaring it 'the finest in the world.' He was especially impressed by the rapid flight of the *kuaka,* the bar-tailed godwit, which would 'test the best marksman.' The beach remained the only reliable land route on the Peninsula until the 1930s when the first inland road was built. Before that, the ten-kilometre crossing on horseback between west and east coasts, over desolate sandy scrub, avoiding treacherous bogs and unstable dunes, was a day's journey.

An Australian racer, Norman 'Wizard' Smith, tested his racing engines on the hard strand; in 1932, he set a world land-speed record on a twenty-five kilometre stretch of wet sand halfway along the tombolo. The following year, Charles Kingsford Smith ran his Fokker Trimotor airplane along the beach 'runway' for the first successful flight across the Tasman to Australia. By that time, the Auckland Aero Club was holding regular weekend flying events on the beach. Later, Te Oneroa-a-Tōhē's long history and local people's wide experience aided preparations for air and sea defence of the west coast during the Second World War when a Japanese invasion was feared.

Nowadays, the annual snapper-fishing contest attracts a thousand anglers and attendance of up to three times that number at the prize giving; hardly surprising with a total prize pool approaching a quarter of a million dollars. For much of the year, tourist buses ply the beach daily on scenic trips to Cape Reinga, while visitors and locals drive to their favourite spots to surf, fish, dive, or simply hang-out with friends. Officially a road, it is not a beach for deckchairs and striped umbrellas. Pedestrians need to watch their backs.

Inevitably all this activity unsettles the fore-dunes. Attempts to stem erosion by planting *pīngao*, the native golden sand sedge, and educating people to use only defined access points is a continuing saga. And though officially protected, *toheroa* – the small clam found only in New Zealand that grows to maturity in the sand, and sustained not only Tōhē and his descendants but a whole canning industry until 1969 – have largely disappeared from the beach.

When the tide is way out, the water's edge forms a fine white pulsing line in the far distance. But a high tide was sloshing around below the dunes when I came to sit here; now it has receded, leaving in front of me a huge expanse of glistening sand, a mirror for the clouds. A few gulls plod contemplatively along the wet sand, eyeing their own reflection before swooping off to settle again a few metres away. While I have been sitting on this clump of marram grass on the fore-dunes, reflecting on the past, the day has faded. I should walk back through the pine plantation before darkness. I stand to brush loose sand from my legs, and stretch them to relieve the stiffness that has set in before skimming down the soft powdery slope to find a firmer path.

For about three hundred metres before the pines begin, I pass between dunes planted as a buffer zone between the sea and the pine plantation. A thin cover of marram and patches of lupins hold the tops of dunes with varying success, but closest to the sea *pīngao* cascades down the sides of dunes and onto the beach above the high tide line. Exotic marram and local *pīngao* live in different relationships to the sand. Marram, with its thick clumps of low-growing milky-blue leaves, pushes deep roots into the sand and relies on short tufted seed heads to spread its offspring. Deposits of new sand encourage the leafy clumps to expand and grow above it, deepening its roots even further.

Pīngao grows in a more open manner that traps wind-blown sand; its vivid green, gold-tinged blades are longer, narrower and serrated, like fine wires bent into graceful curves. In Māori tradition *pīngao* is a *taonga*, a natural treasure, especially valued for weaving. Though *pīngao* produces tan-coloured seed-heads, an additional method of reproduction is more effective in spreading itself. From beneath the plant, stringy jointed rhizomes up to a metre long emerge and wander in all directions, putting up new leaves from each node. As moving sand grains encroach over the stems and hold them in place, the new leaves develop into satellite plants which hold the sand – grass and sand in a cyclical process of holding and binding each other. Beneath the surface, an intricate but fragile lacework of rooted stems maintains the dune to a low undulating profile that will flourish as long as wind-blown sand continues to migrate across the surface. An unfortunate consequence of planting marram as a quicker, easier substitute sand-binder is that *pīngao* is becoming scarce where it once covered whole swathes of dunes; doubly unfortunate in that it is endemic to New Zealand and grows naturally nowhere else.

A hundred metres further inland, where dune surfaces are more stable, the native *toetoe,* or *kākaho*, splays long, ribbed leaves like a pale green fountain, and thrusts up slightly arched banners of cream-coloured feathery seed heads, streaming out in the wind – a smaller and more elegant species of the closely related South American invader, pampas grass. I planted *toetoe* on the Dune and it has thrived wherever it is not overshadowed by trees; it prefers open sunshine. While *pīngao* flourishes in loose sand, *toetoe* needs secure ground to thrive. They do not grow together; each reveals a different landscape. While walking through the dunes I recall a sad little folktale perhaps inspired by this difference.

Pīngao, one of the sea-grass children of the Sea God, Tangaroa, enjoys looking out towards the land. There, beyond the dunes, she sees the waving banners of the brave warrior, Toetoe. She falls in love with strong handsome Toetoe and sends him a message to come closer so that they can be together. He waves in greeting, beckoning to her. When she asks permission of her father to leave the sea and go onto the land, Tangaroa is saddened, and warns her that if she leaves, she will never be able to return. Pīngao gazes with an aching heart at Toetoe, his arching plumes radiant in the setting sun. And she decides to follow her heart and join him. As she emerges from the waves onto the sand, Pīngao calls to Toetoe, but he does not come. Longing to be with him, she struggles onto the dunes beyond the beach. The surface is hot, and she pushes her feet down to the cooler sand beneath. Pīngao calls to Toetoe again, but still he does not come. Realising that she can go no further, Pīngao asks her father to help her, but Tangaroa repeats his earlier warning that he cannot bring her back. To this day, Pīngao remains stranded on the fore-dunes, looking across at Toetoe. He waves to her, but they can never be together.

Though separated in the landscape, *pīngao* and *toetoe* are often woven together in the Māori *tukutuku*, decorative wall panels woven from dried plant stems and leaves to depict *iwi* stories and historical events.

Picking my way between the green fountains of *toetoe* and further into the buffer zone, shrubs and small young trees inhabit dips and hollows where rain water collects. Some are the same native species I am planting on the Dune, and I watch their progress with interest. Shrubs growing in damp creases between dunes grow more lushly than mine, which have to struggle harder for water on a steep, rapidly draining slope. But many plants in the buffer zone are exotics, seeds perhaps brought by the wind, dropped by birds, or carried inadvertently on people's shoes – including a huge spiny cactus. While they all help to hold the sand, they do not recreate the habitats and supportive communities of native vegetation; a realisation that stimulates my thoughts as I walk back through the dim silent pine plantation to my evening tasks on the Dune.

CHAPTER 7

LIFE CYCLES

Walking slowly around the bend of the lake, I pause by the roadside to look up at the Dune. Every imaginable shade of green winks back at me in sunlight that has followed a light shower. Each leaf is part of the magical matrix nurturing uncountable organisms throbbing with life above and below ground.

Twenty summers and winters have passed. There have been brief journeys elsewhere, other books written, additional projects completed. I worked for the Department of Conservation for a while, my remit taking me up and down the length of the tombolo and to the many bays and beaches on the east side as well as the long beach on the west. Despite other interactions, my roots are irretrievably entwined in the Dune.

I push open the old wooden gate by the road and feel drawn in to an ancient story. As I ascend the slope, I walk through secret spaces within a shady green cocoon unseen by the outside world, while the busy community beneath my feet, reaching deep into the belly of the Dune, is invisible to me. Though the larger forest trees whose juvenile shapes differ from their mature form have not yet made their full transition to adulthood, others have grown outward as well as upward, their spread mirrored by the span of their roots below. Their crowns now hold a leaf-laced canopy over the ground, over the paths. The canopy cools the surface and conserves moisture, increasing microclimates with their sub-communities: the diversity that creates within the Dune multiple destinations and life chances.

Bending down to scrape away surface debris, I gather up a pinch of the soil that covers the delicate sand. The texture is still fine, but it is black now with organic matter, and thickening a little each year, especially on the lower parts of the slope where under-surface water gravitates most effectively. And there are worms – a sure sign the soil is improving. Where the tree canopy is complete on these lower sections, mosses and small ferns have found their niches in perpetual twilight. A couple of old, dead tree-fern trunks – *ponga* logs – laid as anchors to hold back the sand beneath plants in the early days, have caught the spirit of the place and wondrously sprung to life, their vivid young fronds emerging half way along the log and overarching the path. Truly, nature's default position is renewal and rebirth.

The middle portion of that 'flat bit at the bottom' is kept in rough grass for working access to the slopes, but during the first year I planted each end with metre-tall seedlings of forest trees; on this favoured and only flat piece of ground, they are now the most matured with their canopies fostering a diverse understorey.

On the western end, where I cut down an old banana clump and left it to rot, the broadleaved *pūriri* has grown to at least ten metres. In spring and summer it bears a mass of carmine nectar-full flowers and bright cerise berries for the birds, and it is already surrounded by its own tiny seedlings pushing their way between the ferns. *Pūriri* is the most passionate tree of my experience. No other tree grows with such ebullient enthusiasm. Sturdy lower limbs stick out at right angles less than a metre from the ground – incidentally offering me a secluded seat under the foliage – while new straight stems spurt up from the middle of branches as well as from the ground until it develops multiple trunks, each of them burgeoning with new sprouts. The tree elbows its way across the whole corner and I have no doubt the roots are doing the same.

Although I no longer climb trees, sitting on a lower branch, bathed in the green luminescence of leaf-screened sunlight, recreates for me the special feeling I experienced as a child of being inside the canopy of a tree. A guest in an inner sanctum – a world apart. One of my favourite hideaways was high up in a chestnut tree whose lower branches swept almost to the ground beneath it, and under whose leafy cover I was invisible. And I confess to the crime of tugging off the biggest green spiky fruits and breaking them open to release the chestnuts before they fell. As long as they were fat with ripeness they made the strongest conkers because they were still supple with moisture, less likely to crack upon impact.

Beside the *pūriri* in that western corner, a *kohekohe*, another broadleaf tree, is managing to rise above the competition. It has flowered for several years; a sight of special delight to me because the flower stalks emerge without leaves straight out of the thin pale bark of the trunk and limbs. The flower panicles grow up to half a metre long, hanging down with the weight of tiny white waxy flowers, both male and female, that mass along their length. When their little seed pods are ripe and brown, they split to reveal two seeds in an unexpected bright scarlet coating. With so many other tasks in my days it is easy to miss this brief florescence which does not occur every year, but I planted two other *kohekohe* on the slope facing the lake and usually manage to catch one or another at its moment of glory.

Things do not always work out as planned, of course, and planting two tree ferns in this corner, right at the bottom of the slope where I thought they would find the most water, proved too optimistic: they flourished for a few years, growing to about three metres before they died. Their thick, black scale-patterned trunks remain to provide habitats for insects and, perhaps one day, they will surge into new life. There are always surprises.

The other day, ignoring the path and scrambling down the slope through the undergrowth – looking for pernicious weeds who no doubt hoped they would not be detected in such cover – I was pulled up sharp by something tough and hard pressing across my throat. Recovering from near throttling, I traced the stem back to the ground. Finding its dark green elongated leaves, I realised that this was a liana, a *kareao* or supplejack vine that I had planted a decade ago and thought long perished. It had grown new shoots. Long, thick mature stems now looped through the understorey and wound around tree trunks, finding their way into the canopy. Up there it might have been displaying its green star-shaped flowers, or red berries, but it was too high for me to see. I moved on, happy to leave it in virile rebirth – no wonder the roots were used in traditional medicine as a tonic.

Supplejack is not the only potential strangler I have to contend with. Cascading down this side of the slope is a string-like native scrambler that has established itself. Thin, lime-green threads turning to gold entwine tightly around stems and branches, anchoring themselves with suckers that penetrate tender young bark to draw on the sap. They do this because they are too deficient in chlorophyll to generate plant sugars through photosynthesis. Though they lack leaves, at intervals along each strand, white flowers smaller than a pinhead produce a seed pod the size of a pea, each containing one round black seed. The wiry threads divide, wind around each other and spread into a mass that looks as if a vast cauldron of spaghetti has been poured over trees, shrubs, even bracken, loose ends flailing in the wind like whip ends to coil around the next leaf or stem in their path. And it is incredibly strong; where this tangle of 'wires' crosses a path, it stops me in my tracks; even a single strand is too strong for me to break it easily by hand; I have to cut them. Even native flora can become a menace. Older trees and shrubs seem to cope with the passage of this parasitic plant, but it can smother and kill young saplings, so I have to control it without eradicating it because it grows only in this region of the country.

The parasite's Māori name, *taihoa*, means 'wait a while'. Whether because it holds you up on the path or because it pauses before eventually spreading on to the next plant I'm not sure, but *taihoa* has come to symbolise the more relaxed attitude to time in the Far North, where a rendezvous at noon can happen anytime within an hour. It reminds me of the unhurried Manx Gaelic saying '*traa de looar*', 'time enough', but is misplaced on the Dune: maintaining natural environments requires as much work as a formal garden.

In the eastern corner of the flat I had planted different species to those in the western corner and the twilight beneath their canopy is of an entirely different character; the light and litter they give to the ground encouraging other possibilities. An ethereal greenness of the atmosphere is pierced on bright mornings by occasional shafts of sunlight that illuminate the structure of leaves, revealing their intricate networks, and glance off rotting, moss-covered tree stumps in which seedlings dare to grow. The air here feels slightly damp, and already bears the sweet-spicy odour of age and decomposition – juicy, earthy, a hint of pepper and a waft of musk.

Dominant are three *kahikatea*, conifers, podocarp that would have grown here thousands of years ago alongside *kauri*. I have to lean right back now to look along their tall straight trunks; at precise intervals, thin frond-like branches carry tiny dark-red-tinted green needles. Despite their height, they are still juveniles and will lose their lower branches over the years, forming smooth trunks as their crowns thicken and widen, eventually growing to a height of sixty-metres. *Kahikatea* are among the oldest of tree species going back almost two-hundred-million years. They were especially valued by Māori for their wood and for their fleshy red and black berries; intrepid harvesters had to climb to twelve or more metres before reaching branches and shaking the fruit into baskets. A hazardous enterprise, recognised in a traditional Māori proverb, or *whakatauki*, quoted by Alan Clarke: '*He toa piki rakau kahikatea, he kai na te pakiaka*' – even the expert tree climber will one day become food for the roots.

I have a special fondness for another resident growing well in the subdued light of this relatively damp corner: the spectacular scrambling *kiekie*, New Zealand's only endemic member of the Pandanus family. Low-lying younger plants flaunt long, narrow shiny-green leaves with finely serrated edges, arching out in all directions like water spouts. Thick aerial roots are already beginning to spread and will allow them to 'walk' over the ground. Older plants have developed stems of two metres or more, and now lean on other plants for support. One has bound itself by its aerial roots all the way up the narrow trunk of an *akeake* nurse tree as if borrowing a spine, its long green streamers emerging along the stem and trailing down its entire length. Traditional weavers collect *kiekie* leaves, prized for making soft, high quality mats and *tukutuku* – the decorative indoor wall panels.

The *kiekie* have all taken many seasons to establish, seeming to wait until the canopy above them spread and the decaying litter on the ground around them thickened. In years ahead, the plants will grow sturdier and clamber up to the tops of trees. Some have remained clustered on the ground in a mass of green sprays; a few years ago, two of these produced their first extraordinary flowers; one plant was male, the other female. The male flower grew five long pale-tan stamens – like cigars – inside thick, fleshy white bracts; when ripe, the pale, greenish female flower cradled three brown, crusty-looking, sausage-sized fruits in pale-pink fleshy bracts. The crusty appearance is caused by hundreds of tiny coated seeds compressed against a woody core. Unfortunately, the male and female flowers did not occur at the same time. More recently, four male flowers appeared on a ground-hugging *kiekie* but there were no flowers on the female plant. Since they flower seldom, I may have to wait a few years for *kiekie* to produce their next flowers, which will, I hope, achieve better coordinated sex lives.

If it seems at times that there is too much 'waiting', there is also so much to look forward to. If not for me personally, for future generations – if we can reverse our abuse of the planet. The land is a living, breathing personality of multiple limbs and organs; we mutilate it at our peril. To view the future in terms of a single fleeting human life is ridiculously out of kilter with earth's natural rhythm. Our artificial concept of time is misleading. Our unrealistic expectation of hours, days, weeks has betrayed us.

Further up the slope, other podocarp are responding well to their natural habitat of light, poor, well-drained ground. Eight young *tōtara* at only five or six metres tall are more untidy than 'mighty'; in their juvenile form, thin branches stick out along the length of the trunk, dividing haphazardly, and all are covered in short stiff bristles of light sage-green. But they are chiefs in the making; traditionally known as 'chiefs of the forest'. *Tōtara's* straight-grained durable wood was favoured for carving out canoes because, if the tree is at least two-hundred years old when felled, its wood will not rot in water. At that age, the heartwood and bark secrete anti-microbial, antioxidant oil – *totarol* – which protects the tree from disease. (It is also extracted as a traditional Māori medicine to relieve fever and skin ailments.)

It is surely a wonderful example of the forests' slow, measured pace of life that the *tōtara* must survive for two centuries before its own medicinal self-care system comes into full operation. And I muse on the reasons for this. After two hundred years, a *tōtara* has finally emerged from adolescence and become a young adult; perhaps, because producing *totarol* requires a lot of energy and effort on the tree's part, nature waits to see which trees are sufficiently strong and established to be worth protecting for the remaining eight hundred or more years of life. Remembering that these podocarp all evolved on Gondwana and grew in the time of dinosaurs, only the tallest and sturdiest would have survived the predations of those voracious clumsy dragons.

In maturity, *tōtara* form a massive trunk up to thirty-metres tall and can live for over a thousand years. It is sobering to realise that when we destroy a mature forest tree, its replacement will take at least eight of our own generations. Yet we seem incapable as a species of planning effectively for even half that timescale. We have raced ahead, speeding everything up, but it cannot last against nature's sure-footed rhythm.

Slow-growing *rimu*, another resin-producing podocarp, whose ancestry goes back seventy million years, goes through a distinctive juvenile phase in separate male and female trees in a similar but more elegant fashion than *tōtara*. The *rimu* I planted on the south slope are only three and four metres tall; their long thin branches, bearing tiny needle-leaves, droop down, draping along the ground and across the path like dark green braids. They are still soft to stroke; with age they will become stiff and rough. Hold aside the tresses, and behind them is a dark red bark that flakes off like strips of tissue paper. In a century or two, the lower branches will have fallen away, leaving the trunk bare and straight; the braids shortened to a sort of crew-cut forming a pyramid-shaped crown. Everything a forest tree does is done slowly, geared for longevity, but *rimu* are slower than most: when cones are finally produced, they take eighteen months for the seeds inside to mature. It is not surprising that *rimu*, too, can live for a thousand years.

Another ancient conifer, the *miro*, grows even more slowly. As an adult, the *miro* bears a massive leafy crown four times the height of its short, sturdy trunk; it is worth noting though, that the height of trees grown in cultivation tends to be less than those in natural forest, where the competition for light among surrounding mature trees is greater. The juveniles on the Dune, mere infants really, have taken sixteen years to grow three metres tall on a single thin trunk bearing droopy, flattened needle-leafed fronds. My project is, indeed, a long-term endeavour; an act of hope and faith. Yet there is constant inspiration and reward. And it eases my impatience that I can gaze at a slope growing brave saplings and precocious shrubs and 'see' them as they will be in ten, fifty, or a hundred year's time.

One of the advantages of living on top of steep slopes is the ability to look into the tops of trees. Of special delight is *rewarewa*, New Zealand Honeysuckle, an endemic, broadleaf evergreen of the Proteaceae family that can grow to thirty metres tall. The first *rewarewa* I planted on the north-facing slope, directly below my cottage, is now at least eight metres tall. The long, vermillion flowers with tightly curled petals and bright yellow stamens that hang from the branches in spring like ringlets, and are set off at the very top against a cerulean sky, are directly in my line of sight from the veranda. During summer, the flowers give way to long velvety-brown seed pods which, when they break open to let out their two winged seeds, look like tiny canoes.

A source of great joy to me is that strong young *kauri* trees have now grown tall enough to gaze over the burial ground of their ancient ancestors in the swamp. Around them, I planted species of small trees, shrubs and grasses that I noted growing in a conserved *kauri* grove in the Mangamuka hills – the 'eye brows' that etch the horizon behind the almond-eyed lake. Over millennia of evolution, *kauri* forests created their own distinctive community of flora and fauna – their natural companions. On the south side of the Dune, other young *kauri* trees contemplate the lake beneath whose glistening waters rest more ghosts of their forebears.

The first-planted *kauri*, and the tallest, is approximately twenty-five years old – allowing a few years for her growth to a one-metre seedling in a nursery before I planted her. Last year, she grew her first small cone – just one, a female cone that resembles a pale-green golf ball – and has produced at least three more this year (I say 'she' out of natural bias: *kauri* are hermaphrodite, bearing both male and female cones – male cones are brown and elongated). Two or three lower branches have already been cast off and, where some minor trauma has broken a patch of thin silvery bark, the first globule of soft milky gum has appeared to seal and heal the abrasion. Early Māori settlers collected fresh resin for chewing gum, but I leave it in place, feeling an unaccountable and unearned parental pride and excitement in the young *kauri's* achievement.

Such feelings are inevitably accompanied by a sense of responsibility and the concern that it generates. And there is good cause for anxiety over *kauri*. In 2006, in the Waitakere Range, along the west coast of central North Island, long-established *kauri* trees began to die of an unknown disease. Grim white skeletons spiked the skyline where these mighty monarchs had thrived for centuries. The disease began to spread.

Three years of research later, the cause of 'kauri dieback' was discovered to be a pathogen which scientists named *Phytophthera agathidicida* – literally, 'kauri-killing fungi'. A higher-order mould than the potato blight, which nonetheless caused the Irish famine and devastated the land, it operates in a way similar to all fungi. Microscopic inert spores lurk in the soil until the right level of warmth and dampness enables their transformation into mobile zoospores, whose tails enable them to migrate through moisture to seek out their prey: *kauri* tree roots.

Once attached to the root hairs, the zoospores produce tiny hollow threads, mycelia, which penetrate the trees living tissue. Mycelia form a massive web inside the base of the tree, generating more spores that disperse into the soil, and blocking and consuming all the water and nutrients coming up through the roots. As a result, the *kauri* trees starve to death. Mature trees may take decades to die, the process not detected for several years. Even if it were, there is no known cure. And prevention is hampered by incomplete knowledge of how static resting spores spread from one forest to another; *kauri* groves can be isolated from humans tramping soil on their boots from one area to another, but additional agents are likely involved that cannot be so readily controlled.

Why these zoospores target *kauri* roots and how they recognise them is, as yet, a mystery. To do so successfully, they would have to overwhelm existing networks of beneficial root fungi, and perhaps it is these other fungi that are sensed and lead the zoospores to their quarry. In nature's flow and flux nothing is ever certain; nothing can be taken for granted. In a sense, this uncertainty urges the creative energy of the earth and its ecosystems; creative energy that humanity must apply to redress the unthinking damage of our past and present generations. Uncertainty not stasis is the generator of life and innovation. In Rainer Maria Rilke's disarmingly simple phrase: 'Life is lived in transition.'

Around juvenile forest giants now growing on the Dune, most of the supporting cast of broadleaf woodland trees, shrubs, ferns, climbers and grasses that I planted – all the other sons and daughters of Tāne – continue to play their roles, each at its own pace. Among them is pigeonwood, *porokaiwhiri;* the only other tree I have seen to come close to the *pūriri's* rampant vigour. A small, upland forest-edge tree, pigeonwood puts out multiple, smooth slender trunks; some curve around each other, and where they touch and rub, they join together in a messy orgy of self-hugs. They, too, are surrounded by their massed seedlings of equal verve and determination, though few, if any, of these seedlings will survive in the shadow and competition of their parent. But birds gorge on the bright orange berries, especially the *kererū* or *kūkupa*, the native wood pigeon, and spread seeds further afield. Several strong saplings of such bird-sown pigeonwood are now growing on the south-facing slope.

I have already described a few other species of the supporting cast of smaller trees and shrubs. Their number is large, each enriching the forest story with its own character, lines, and costume – flowers of many shapes and shades; fruits of all colours; leaves wavy, red-tinged, blotched, veined, pale, golden, long, broad, soft, or hard; stems and trunks polished, scaled, sculptured, arched or straight – and many with special gifts to heal. Because a lot of these plants are endemic to New Zealand – growing naturally nowhere else – rather than write pages of 'credits' here, I have listed in an Appendix all the species planted on the Dune and the roles they play in nature's theatre.

Their diversity takes on special significance in the face of unexpected diseases and rapid changes in climate: I cannot foresee which species will survive in the long term, but barring complete devastation, the most adaptable among them will continue. And even within a single species, genetic variation among individuals will enable some to adapt better than others to changing circumstances.

The significance of seed dispersal on the Dune by birds and wind is that, with each naturally germinated seed, there is a chance of slight variation through genetic mutations. Most mutations are entirely insignificant, but sometimes they result in differences in leaf or flower colour or shape, and it is always possible that a variation gives a plant an advantage in resilience. If a naturally germinated seedling is growing in a place where it is likely to thrive, I keep an eye on it to make sure it is not smothered or accidentally crushed. If they are growing in too challenging a spot – too close to the parent tree for example – I remove them and grow them on to be planted elsewhere on the Dune.

I mentioned in an earlier chapter the book, *The Hidden life of Trees* by German forester, Peter Wohlleben. Since 2017 when an English translation was published, this fascinating read has occupied dark winter evenings and explained much of my own experience in watching the five acre forest come to life over the years. His overarching message is that a forest is much more than the number of its trees: it is an integrated organic entity of its own; a complex ecosystem woven by interdependent organisms below ground and above it; a discreet 'conurbation' of forest margins and 'city centre', built as much on cooperation as competition. There is a lesson here that we humans should heed: it is not the fitness of individuals that determines survival, but the strength of the community of which they are a part. Like a tower of playing-cards, to remove one part disrupts the whole.

Like any complex system, a forest's establishment and operation depends on effective communication – passing on vital information, sharing resources, and supporting mutual defence. Much has still to be learned and, by definition, such discoveries require a long time-scale, but Wohlleben quotes ongoing research into how this communication among trees works through exchanges of electrical impulses and chemical agents. Ahead in this research is Suzanne Simard, Professor of forest ecology at the University of British Columbia, whose book, *Finding the Mother Tree,* is published this year.

I have already mentioned critical exchanges that take place at a microscopic level between fungi and tree roots within dark regions below the ground, but others take place above the surface between trees and between them and the creatures that live on and around them.

For example, many trees defend themselves from excessive insect attacks by secreting a toxin into their leaves that deters or even kills insects and other browsers. Chemicals in the browser's saliva alert the tree to its presence, and the tree responds by pulsing out the toxin through its sap. At the same time, it might pump out an odour to warn nearby trees – a system similar to ants' and bees' use of pheromones to exchange information. The process may take several hours (apparently, sap and signals pass inside a tree at the rate of about one centimetre per minute), so it does not prevent insect attack but reduces the extent of damage. Presumably, a focus on damage limitation, rather than prevention, is a trade-off between protection and the costs of defence: to maintain toxins permanently pumped through its leaves would divert too much of the tree's energy from its prime purpose: to grow. A stressed or weak tree will therefore be less effective in defending itself. This is borne out on the Dune, where the most signs of insect mischief are seen on plants coping with more challenging conditions than others.

This defence process might explain the limited amount of damage by looper moth caterpillars that I see regularly on one of the species thriving on the Dune. *Kawakawa* is an understorey shrub or small tree whose dark jointed stems sprawl among other plants, using them to support its mass of vivid green heart-shaped leaves and pollen-covered flower spikes that look like short, downside-up catkins. There may be half a dozen bites taken out of a few leaves, but I have not seen damage severe enough to seriously threaten the plant.

Every part of the *kawakawa* shrub provides ingredients for traditional medicine, especially for skin conditions, pain relief, and a general tonic – though toxic if overused. A late nineteenth century botanist even recorded its value as an aphrodisiac. *Kawakawa* was also burned in food gardens because the smoke killed insects. Modern science identifies the main active chemical as *myristicine*, an anti-bacterial, a natural insecticide, and in some forms, a mild narcotic; it is part of the phenol family, found also in nutmeg and parsley. Folk wisdom advises that the best time to collect *kawakawa* is after the leaves have been bitten by caterpillars. As a tree's defence system, *myristicine* in the leaves would be at its most potent following initial insect attack. That traditional healers wait for the first caterpillar bites before gathering the plant reveals an engaging insight into human participation in the forest community.

Equally significant in Wohlleben's work is recognition of the time taken to form the networked community of a forest. More than a hundred years is required for the thousands of fungi, algae and bacteria to complete the cycles of decay and transformation that create soil to support a forest. On the Dune, the soil started virtually from scratch as loose sand. Most of the work of soil formation is hidden below ground, but on the surface I see signs of these relationships beginning.

Lichen – a symbiotic union between fungi and algae – already decorate the limbs of young trees with frilly blued-silver bracelets, and outline others with lengths of crisp tangled 'hair'. On the wider space of trunks, they have created unique mandalas with amazing mathematical precision. Within their exact perimeters, a chaos of seemingly random curls and swirls lie stiff like brawling surf frozen in place; sometimes they are stained with traces of red, black or yellow. Mosses and lichens do the trees no harm, quite the reverse: algae fix nitrogen from the air which rain washes down into the soil.

The rata vine, cousin to *pōhutukawa*, its tiny round leaves crowding dark wiry stems that branch off in all directions, already covers the surface of much of the south-facing slope, and has begun to clothe the trees, inching up and around their bark. One day in the long future they will bear flowers: tiny cups of nectar fringed with long red or white stamens, giving them the appearance of fluffy pompoms. In the meantime, the spreading vine helps to bind the surface, protects the ground from erosion, and holds moisture in the soil. And the visible signs of fungi busy below ground – their impetuous fruiting bodies bursting through the surface – increase each year. Though trees dominate, the warp and weft of multiple other lives begin to fill out and enrich the forest tapestry.

In a chapter of Wohlleben's book headed 'Tree School', I find support for my stinginess with water. Writing of Sitka spruce forests on Germany's rocky mountainsides, the conditions Wohlleben describes – the all-year limited availability of water and its seasonal scarcity – is echoed in the Dune. Sitka exercise restraint in their daily use of water and learn to store it within their cells against shortages; trees growing in these conditions grow more slowly, are more resilient, and live longer than those leading more flamboyant lives where water is plentiful. (An unbidden image pops into my head of celebrities leading fast lives in the world's plush watering-holes where over-indulgence may threaten health and longevity.) On the Dune, young trees on rationed water learn to push their roots further into the ground in search of moisture as well as to store it during drought. But it is a fine balance; I sometimes get it wrong and lose a seedling, especially during droughts when the water tank is low.

Shade has a related effect on the speed of growth and hardiness; with less light, photosynthesis is reduced, growth is slower, and less water is needed. The role of pioneer nurse-trees such as *akeake* and tea tree to provide light shade is critical to the survival of planted seedlings. As they grow and need more space, I trim back over-attentive nurses who threaten to smother their charges. Eventually, the young forest tree outstrips its attendants and takes their place, creating shade for understorey plants and its own seedlings while shading out competition.

We have long known that trees monitor and make individual adjustments in response to changes in soil, air, water and light. And there is now no doubt trees are aware of and respond to each other as well as to other living organisms affecting them above and below ground. It is an intriguing thought that trees might even be aware of our own animal presence: the vibrations of our tread over their root zones; the odours of our skin and clothes; pulses given off from our magnetic fields. Little is known of human pheromones and electrical signals in interacting with nature. The full extent of tree communication and intelligence has yet to be discovered in this necessarily slow but vital field of research. Whether it can keep ahead of the pace at which primary forests are being destroyed is another matter.

I was approaching the halfway mark of work on the Dune when I received one of those middle-of-the-night phone calls from the other side of the world that always herald disturbing news. My aged but normally robust mother was suddenly, seriously, ill. I bullied my way onto a flight leaving within twenty-four hours, and went straight to the hospital on arrival. It was not the first crisis to call me back in all the years I had lived and worked around the world. But it turned out to be the last. After a six-week struggle as I sat by her bed, my mother was too exhausted to hold on to life.

From the start, Ma had followed the Dune's progress through letters, photographs and my annual visits, and I decided to create something special on the Dune in her memory. I had removed the few self-sown pine trees on the slope overlooking the swamp to make way for native plants – except one: an old radiata pine in which the herons like to roost. It had never been pruned but had clearly survived some major traumas in its long life. The circumference of its sturdy trunk is almost four metres, some of which is taken up by thick scales of bark, but the trunk only extends at that width for about six metres. It must have lost its growing tip at some time because, beyond that point, five heavy limbs, each as thick as a young pine tree, radiate from the centre; a sixth limb, the same size as the others, has taken on the role of leader to form a new vertical trunk. And barely another metre up, six more limbs emerge in every direction. All of these side branches curve outward for several metres before growing up towards the light. Having spent much of my childhood half-way up trees, this second set of radiating limbs looked like a tree hug, an inviting cradle, and I decided to have a simple tree house built in it with a small legacy Ma had left me.

The tree 'house' is a modest affair, more like an eagle's eyrie: two sets of steps, divided by a landing, lead up to a five-sided planked platform framed by a palisade of tea tree stakes, the whole covered by a green sail. Bench seats along two sides flank a wooden table –

free-standing when wind and herons permit. The tree house is partly suspended from robust limbs and partly leaning on others to spread the weight. It was designed by an arbourist to disturb the tree as little as possible: the whole structure flexes to the branches' own movements with the gentle creaks and sighs of a woody refrain – the lullaby of an old sailing barque. This became my special place for thinking, for editing, for watching *pūkeko* rootle in the recovering wetland during the day, and witnessing the sun slipping below the horizon at night. And herons still roosted there when the mood took them.

Today, I stand at the rail of the tree house looking out over a changed landscape. No *pūkeko*. No occasional *kuaka* landing for a quick travel snack. No frogs yodelling their midday chorus. And the harrier hovers less often over ground that supports so little life. The swamp, the wetland, has been utterly destroyed.

Nine years ago, a battalion of heavy excavators and earth movers advanced across the wetland on caterpillar tracks, crushing everything in their path. Sent to hunt ancient *kauri* for the export trade, they dug yawning pits into the peat to exhume the bodies of huge trees that had lain there for fifty thousand years. Deep ditches were cut around the periphery of the swamp, and for months, pumps droned day and night sucking away the water – the wetland's lifeblood.

Soon, the whole area was littered with excavated

kauri remains, and heavy lifters began to load them onto massive trucks. One shortened tree trunk was so heavy, its diameter so huge, that it took an entire day to manoeuvre it onto a truck. Its weight required sole occupation of a thirty-wheeled flat-bed trailer. As the loaded vehicle thundered along the lane between the swamp and the Dune, I felt the vibration through the wooden floor of my cottage sixty metres above.

By the end of that summer, although the deepest pits remained, bulldozers had levelled the ground to a lumpy surface that has sunk at least two metres lower than it had originally been. It remains a seasonally boggy stretch of rough ground with patches of reedy grasses, where blanketing gorse is kept at bay only by regular spraying of herbicide, and where hordes of mosquitoes breed – their buzzing the only living sound. The long term damage may be more extensive. It seems likely that the deepest pit – at approximately eight metres – broke through the hard pan that holds subsurface water. If this is the case, water will be drained away permanently and, as the whole swamp has sunk, if the broken pan is now at a lower level than it is beneath the lake, water will slowly be drained from the lake and lost forever.

Even the dead are silenced: the irreplaceable *taonga* of the past, and the knowledge that paleoecologists could have gained from *kauri* tree rings, pollen and other traces of ancient life – all now lost.

The future of other Sweetwater Lakes looks more positive. All the lakes are monitored by environmental authorities. Plans have been drawn up to deal with pollutants and invasive species and, where necessary, perimeter fences erected to stop cattle trampling the margins. The six *iwi*, or tribes, of the Aupōuri Peninsula – *Muriwhenua*, 'the end of the land', i.e. 'the tail of the fish' – each with their own war stories of past conflict between them, have jointly launched a consultative initiative to preserve the natural, cultural, and ecological heritage of the area. It began with a detailed assessment of all these features, including those in the Sweetwater Lakes, entitled 'Te Māke – a land of floating islands, moving hills, taniwha, and heroes'. Their cooperation augurs well for a future that will contain many challenges, among them, that of the climate emergency.

Other small developments also help. Motorised craft and jet skis – which previously chased each other crazily around, churning up the sediment — are no longer allowed on the almond-eyed lake; a low barrier of wooden stumps at the water's edge prevents the boats being launched and, incidentally, stops thoughtless off-road drivers and fishers from driving into the lake to wash salt and contaminating debris from their vehicles.

As I was writing this final chapter, the Dune experienced the most severe drought it has had to endure. No significant rain fell for the six months of summer and spring, while temperatures on my veranda ranged between twenty-five and thirty-four degrees centigrade. Rain clouds hovered at times on the horizon and drifted passed. Areas to the south and east received rain while our portion was a drifting mist; at best, light showers lasting minutes. No cattle grazed the parched sandhills;

there was nothing for them to eat; their hooves would simply churn the ground to dust. Elderly residents said that the last drought as severe as this was over forty years ago, hinting that it was a once-in-a-lifetime event, but old weather patterns and expectations no longer hold. There is no reason why this drought could not be repeated next year or the year after.

On the near-side shore of the lake, water shrank from its margins revealing old *kauri* stumps and trunks that have never been visible before, even in previous droughts. In the still of night a new marsh smell rose from the lake, the fetid odour of decaying vegetation. For at least a hundred metres out from the lake shore, the mud was dry enough to walk on; beyond that, clumps of sedge sat in a couple of inches of water, insufficient to sustain them for long. Committees of Caspian terns sat in semi-circles on exposed logs, beaks to the wind, enjoying a newly accessible feeding ground. Other sharp eyes saw the same opportunity. In daily circuits of the Dune, the harrier glided low over the muddy flat looking for unattended nests and small prey; the terns rose in white flapping panic, returning only after the harrier had left the area.

Merciless heat affects beach life too. During one week in the midst of the drought, young mussels and other shell fish died in their tens of thousands, carpeting the sand with an image of Armageddon. A westerly wind brought the stench of rotting seafood to hover around the Dune.

A light breeze often makes the air feel cooler but it

dries out plants and soil even faster. In most cases, if a tree that is more than two or three metres tall shows signs of severe thirst, it is already too late to help it because it would require tens of gallons of water a day. Some may survive through the summer without showing much outward signs of stress, but if their root hairs and tips have dried out and begun to shrivel, they would need a wet winter followed by a few wet summers for their roots to recover. Without that, they are likely to struggle for a year or two and die quite suddenly.

Summer droughts will become longer and drier as the climate heats further. I have to select which of the youngest seedlings to support with watering. I want them all to survive, of course, but it is inevitable that the Dune's adaptation to a hotter drier climate will result in some changes in species. Those that have been 'only just managing' during the last twenty years are unlikely to adjust further.

Heart-breaking though it is, I achieve nothing for the long-term health of this small forest by maintaining plants that will become entirely dependent on my intervention. Throughout the drought, I watered only the seedlings and saplings which are most likely to adapt to drier conditions once they are established. One thought that gave me some comfort was that *kauri* forests and their associated flora have survived through warmer climates in the past. Estimates of temperatures over millennia may be unreliable, but are much less so for the period since the last retreat of polar ice – the Holocene. Ten thousand years ago, average temperatures in New Zealand are believed to have been about one degree centigrade higher than they are now, a pattern that lasted some four thousand years and during which forests flourished. To stay positive, I kept careful note of which species coped best in each part of the Dune, so that when the drought ended, I could replace lost trees and shrubs with those more robust species.

Light, brief showers began at intervals at the end of June and continued, with a little more volume in July. This was fortunate because, not only were plants given some relief with surface water, but it allowed the ground to absorb water gradually: sudden heavy rain after drought cannot penetrate the soil and runs off, causing erosion and land-slips. By mid July, the ground was damp for only a couple of inches below the surface, and though water glistened over the lake margins and clouds again drifted across the surface, it was barely deep enough to cover a *pūkeko's* ankles. But when storms and heavy rain arrived over the following weeks, the ground was ready to absorb it and, as soon as the skies cleared, I began to survey the state of my woody domain.

My optimism for the *kauri* was misplaced. Seven youngsters who had grown to three or four metres did not survive; five taller, older *kauri* – including my 'first-planted' pride and joy – appear to have weathered the drought, although this will not be certain for a couple of years. These were the heaviest losses, repeated on many properties in the area with better soils, so the cause was not simply the challenges of the Dune. All the *rimu* and other conifers coped well; among broadleaf trees only one or two were lost from any species group – isolated victims in difficult places.

When trees and shrubs are challenged by drought their response is often gradual, but the struggle is real as the force to live causes each plant to work through its options. Typically a tree begins with dropping lower, older leaves to sustain newer growth; tender growing tips may die next, to allow more mature leaves to continue functioning; then whole branches might die one at a time; finally, nothing is left but a bare stem or trunk. Even so, some trees have not given up entirely. I had forgotten the thin, dry trunk and remaining shrivelled leaves of a young red *matipou* until well after the drought had passed – there was so much other work to do. Imagine my delight one day to see tiny red growing tips emerging from several places along the trunk. Established *matipou* often put up new shoots from the roots, forming multi-trunked trees, and there is a strong possibility that this determined little tree will do the same once it grows enough leaves to create the necessary energy. Never be too hasty with the undertaker's axe.

Of necessity, the planting season began a month late and everything was watered-in thoroughly. Learning from experience, I planted only two new *kauri* seedlings and in places that could be easily watered in the future, replacing the others with *toru* and *rewarewa*: two species that had managed well throughout the drought. I also arranged for another rainwater tank to be installed; half the size of the main tank, but sufficient to give me a little more leeway for watering new plantings when, rather than if, such a drought is repeated. These last few weeks have felt like the earlier days of vegetating the Dune, rootling around for the best spot for a seedling, digging, supporting, nurturing. And I am raising cuttings and seeds in the shade house again, but only in small numbers. It brings back the feelings of trust, hope and concern amid uncertainty because my role on nature's stage is limited and my control non-existent. It will be vital to hold fast to trust and hope through this coming year when a second drought in forecast. For my own welfare, I must accept the limits of my interventions and develop a degree of detachment – hard though that is.

Curiously, the Dune feels larger than when I first scrambled up its wounded flanks. My mind-map has increased the distances, expanded the possibilities between one point and another.

The bird population of regular residents and visitors has expanded, too. I can practically mark my day by the appearances of long-standing residents: kingfishers commute daily from sand burrows to the lake, ever watchful; a wary *tūī* chortles from a high branch as I pass below, his white bow-tie quivering; little white-eyes swarm on berry bushes; blackbirds and thrushes dig up the mulch; herons pace long branches of the tree-house pine, shoulders hunched, mumbling like grumpy judges discussing a difficult case; sparrows try their chances everywhere; and little fantails follow my every move.

The harriers do not breed on the Dune, but it is part of their daily hunting circuit along with the lake and the swamp.

Less easily visible, bush wrens, rifleman, and grey warblers nest in the canopies lower down the south slope, while California quail and secretive pheasants occasionally nest on the north-facing slope. And the 'morepork' call of the native owl, *ruru*, sweetens the night air less often than I would wish.

Among the migrants and visitors, parrots (the Australian eastern rosella) and our native woodpigeons, *kererū* or *kūkupa*, visit to gorge their fill of autumn's fruitfulness, shining cuckoo come to leave their orphan eggs in spring, and flights of welcome swallows swing through the air scooping up insects on late summer evenings. Less welcome are the raucous gangs of Indian mynah birds and Australian magpies, the bullies of open woodland country. Magpies, in particular, have a reputation for raiding native birds' nests to feed on their eggs and chicks, and they harass smaller birds from perching and foraging – behaviour suggested in their name: *Artamidae tyrannica*. Their presence is the result of one of those naive attempts to outdo nature at her own game: Australian magpies were deliberately introduced to New Zealand in the nineteenth century to control insect pests. Little research has been carried out into their true impact on native birds, but they are no match for our *tūī*. I have seen a pair of *tūī* perch above a magpie, watch it closely for some minutes and, pouncing in unison, chase it out of the tree.

One of the reasons so many birds now flourish on the Dune is the busy buzzy insect population. In addition to the celebrated cicadas and mantids, numberless other creatures crawl on the ground, feed on plants or flit through the air: shrill grasshoppers, jewel-coloured dragonflies, mosquitoes, aphids, bees and wasps, moths, beetles and butterflies of every description, spiders large and small, more kinds of fly than I can recognise, and zillions of ants. The latter provide a filling diet for tiny shiny lizards (skinks) the colour of chocolate and no longer than my finger from nose to tail-tip, who zap through leaf litter and around plant pots, and often pop out from cool corners in my cottage – another cooperative house-mate. Less companionable are the black shiny beetles that lurk in dark crevices of old wood; if I accidentally step on one, it emits a nauseating sulphurous stench of death and rot that is quite overwhelming.

The initial work of installing paths and steps, and the bulk of propagation and planting completed in the first decade – solely with my own labour – took a physical toll. Since then, I appreciate occasional help with heavier tasks: repairing steps, felling, and the back-breaking job of pulling everlasting gorse and wattle seedlings – though their numbers are noticeably decreasing – but the painstaking task of distributing precious water during drought remains mine alone.

There is more time now to observe and wonder as I linger among the plants. My fingers trace the contours of rough-barked trees, stroke the silken finish of others, and gently caress leaves as I pass, feeling their fine serrations, their glossy strength – careful in my reverie to avoid the long, arching blades of well-named cutty grass whose razor-sharp edges can inflict a deep wound. And everywhere I go, I hear the chi-chi-chi of *kōtare*, the sacred kingfisher, and I am followed by the little *pīwakawaka*, the fantail, flashing back and forth to gobble up the insects my tread disturbs.

An early riser, I love to witness the colours of dawn when the sun opens like a vast cosmic flower. Though I try to capture these moments in my camera, photography can be a distraction: technology allows us to amass spectacular images, but the inner vision they evoke is best held in the memory. In the evening, when the sun appears low in the sky, I leave whatever I am doing to watch its gentle descent, gilding the lake, trees, hills, clouds – everything the glowing light touches, until gold turns to rubies and the deeper hues of garnets. And often, I am held there in the darkness by the cooling air and the sounds of night that replace vision with new perceptions. The cackle of stiff puka leaves agitated by a breeze; brief furtive scuttles in the undergrowth; the murmurings of invisible birds settling for the night; the plink of raindrops falling through the canopy; and, on a lucky night, the urgent call for 'morepork' from an owl hunting for supper.

Each day I find new treasure around my feet and above my head. I have become a sky-watcher. Polynesian explorers called New Zealand the land of 'Aotearoa', 'The Long White Cloud', and from my pivotal view on top of the Dune I see not only long white clouds, but a morphing series of fascinating cloud formations that excite the imagination. Heroes in wheeled chariots may be chasing dragons over the lake, while on the other side, angels dance over the sandhills. At night, centaurs, bulls, lions, and scorpions rule as well as a charioteer: in the absence of city lights and in the clarity of the surrounding Pacific Ocean, I have a splendid view of the stars on a clear night.

Some of the Polynesian seafarers' names for the stars have been handed down through the generations attached to myths and legends. To Māori astronomers, the Southern Cross – the South Celestial Pole – is Te Puna, the Anchor that held Maui's *waka* while he fished, and is tethered to Te Pātiki, the dark rock, otherwise known as the Coal Sack – the dark nebula of dust alongside the Southern Cross that obscures part of the Milky Way. The fishhook with which Maui caught the tail of the fish and raised North Island out of the sea is there, too. Te Matau a Maui, 'Maui's Fish Hook', is represented in Scorpius – incidentally, my own star sign.

Though I never cease to marvel at nature's wonders and revelations on the patch of earth I have made my responsibility, gazing into our own galaxy, aware that it occupies such a tiny part of the universe, brings an invigorating sense of perspective on sleepless, hot summer nights. However fleeting our presence within this vastness, it *is* a presence, and it can be a small force for good if we make it so.

The people who said 'you will never do it'; 'you need lawns'; 'you should have built on the flat bit at the bottom', now ask, 'But aren't you lonely on that hill of yours?' How could I be lonely in such company, such diversity, such constant change of light and sound and form, and so much still to discover?

The Dune is stronger for its journey, now bound by generations of migrating roots below the surface, and protected by a spreading warp and weft of limbs above ground. I am stronger anchored to this land. At peace with who I am, I contemplate with calm acceptance my physical mortality, my speck of existence, a single grain of sand within a vast time-space. Each of us sees and feels our surroundings differently; our appreciation of each place determines our relationship with it. And the reciprocations we engage in change both.

The Dune and its neighbouring lake and swamp and beach are real enough, but it is not specific locations and names that are significant in this narrative. It is 'place'. Place is a process, an experience unique to each individual's perception and emotions; my 'place' is not the same as your 'place' even at the same location. Location tells us only where; it is impersonal, inanimate. Place poses the questions when, how, why and for whom; we act within it, become part of it. And places impact people, physically and psychologically, as my work on the Dune affects me. Everything that has happened here since its deep-time formation has seeped into the culture, into the land and into the people. I am surrounded by the story of place as I interweave the threads of my own story.

A location has a misleading sense of permanence, of

stasis; the feeling that we see a situation which has always been here and will remain after we have left – a conclusion that 'this is how it is' when, in reality, it is merely our perception in a slice of time. We tend to do the same when we meet people for the first time, reducing them to our first impressions. All life is a process of becoming; of natural forces in flow and flux, in a state of constant change and movement. In this story, I have tried to capture a sense of the current of transformation which is evident in studying the past and essential in dealing with the present and the future. A future we will survive only if we make the transformations in our lives necessary to adapt to a world changing with unprecedented speed.

Are our travels over, then, our journey complete? Have the Dune and I become settlers, no longer migrants? Viewed from a wider perspective, migration is a perpetual state. Nothing is truly permanent, neither trees nor sand dunes. Looking back over the millennia that formed the dunes, the swamp, the beach, recalling the sea ancestors and the volcanic ancestors, there is no 'solid earth'. And I realise that our 'for-ever-and-ever' is but a limited span we cannot foresee. Land and people exist within a process of transition because stasis is a form of death. In this sense, we are all travellers on journeys towards a state of becoming; each of us a moving, transforming originality; our final form and destination unknown.

I am not sure whether I adopted the Dune or the Dune adopted me, or which of us has most affected the other. When we first met, the Dune was as ill-equipped for its new static role inland, away from its beach origins, as I was for a settled life after wandering the globe. But my role here has changed. Like a guardian whose ward has come of age, I have become more a companion than an active accomplice – the Dune no longer needs my interventions, or less so. Intricate life continues within its invisible silent spaces generating energy that echoes up to the surface. But the Dune's time-span is far greater than mine and it needs security.

I have planted trees whose maturity I will never see because without faith in a future there *is* no future. As individuals, we may feel powerless to make changes to the present, and yet, almost every action we take, consciously and unconsciously, affects our built and natural environment. We have the power to make those actions positive in a multitude of ways. In the spaces between putting the Dune's story together, I have set up a charitable trust to come into operation to maintain this five acre forest when I am no longer here to keep the Dune company. The land and buildings will be available as community educational and health resources focused on native woodland. In an appropriate spirit of optimism, the Trust is designed to last 'in perpetuity' – however long that may be.

Sitting on the veranda on still evenings I hear waves churning the beach – it sounds like a distant freight train passing for eternity. Inevitably, the sea will rise to claim again the sandhills it created so many eons ago. Perhaps only the Dune's feet will be inundated and it will stand, an emerald-clad island overlooking the lapping waters.

We have both been transfigured, migrants made ready for an unknowable future. And soon, my ashes will nurture the soil – my last reciprocation.

GLOSSARY

Akeake*: (Dodonaea viscosa)* small coastal and forest-edge tree, a pioneer in scrub.

Atua*:* a god or principal spiritual force in Māori cosmology, especially of natural elements involved in the creation of the natural world and its inhabitants.

Cabbage trees: *ti kouka*, a general common name for various species of *Cordyline*.

Cicada: insect of the *Cicadoidea* family, emitting a characteristically shrill song.

Coprosma: genus of tropical evergreen trees and shrubs with large variety of natural and cultivated species.

Corokia*: korokio,* genus of evergreen tropical shrubs of six natural species and numerous hybridised cultivars.

Dab chick: (*Poliocephalus rufopectus),* w*eiweia,* New Zealand grebe, endemic, rare and threatened.

Endemic: existing naturally nowhere else.

Fantail: *piwakawaka, (Rhipidura fuliginosa),* common small brown bird with white eyebrows and chinstrap; displays long black and white tail feathers in a fan shape.

Flax: harakeke, (Phormium spp) tall perennial plant with long sword-shaped leaves used for weaving baskets, mats, ropes. Entirely different to European flax used for weaving linen.

Gondwana: a huge plate of earth's crust in the southern hemisphere that broke up into the present southern continents some 200 million years ago.

Grey warbler: *(Gerygone igata)* small grey-brown bird with pearly grey front and underside.

Harakeke: Māori name for flax plant *(Phormium tenax)*, the leaves important for weaving.

Harrier: (*Circus approximans gouldi*) bird of prey, hunts in open country, nests in swamps and scrub.

Hebe: shrub or small tree of which New Zealand has over a hundred species.

Iwi: Depending on context: an identified social group in Māori, a 'people', a tribe or confederation of tribes.

Inanga: (*Galaxius maculates*), smallest of the whitebait species of fish.

Kānuka: *(Kunzea ericoides)* shrub or tree with tiny pin-like aromatic leaves, several species, often conflated with *mānuka,* commonly referred to as tea tree.

Karakia: Māori prayer, blessing, or ritual chant.

Kauri: *(Agathis australis)* large forest conifer, podocarp, up to 50 metres, resinous, endemic to New Zealand, can live up to 4000 years.

Kawakawa: *(Macropiper spp.)*, pepper tree, deciduous shrub or small tree with heart-shaped leaves, used in traditional Māori medicine.

Kiekie: *(Freycinetia banksii)*, tropical scrambling climber of the Pandanaceae family.

Kikuyu grass: (*Pennisetum clandestinum*), invasive East African scrambling grass.

Kingfisher: *(Todiramphus sanctus vagans)*, this New Zealand species has pink breast feathers.

Kōtare: Te Reo Māori name for kingfisher.

Kōwhai: *(Sophora spp)* semi-deciduous decorative tree with vivid yellow pendulous flowers, grows to 20 metres, eight species endemic to New Zealand.

Kuaka: Bar-tailed godwit, *(Limosa lapponica)*, large, long-beaked wader, seasonal migrant to New Zealand, breeding in Alaska.

Kuia: grandmother, or female elder, source of wisdom and traditional knowledge.

Kumara: sweet potato, staple crop in traditional agriculture.

Kumarahou: *(Pommaderris kumeraho)*, golden tainui, a pioneering scrubland shrub; its leaves lather when rubbed in water, giving it the nickname 'gum-diggers soap'.

Kuta: *(Eleocharis sphacelata)*, freshwater grass-like plant with long tough leaves, sedge.

Looper moth caterpillar: *(Cleora scriptaria)*, specific to *kawakawa* shrub (*Macropiper* spp.)

Machair: fertile grassland on sandy coastal fringes mainly in north-west Scotland and Ireland.

Magpie: (Australian magpie – *Artamidae tyrannica*), introduced into New Zealand 1864-1874 to control insect pests.

Mahoe: *(Melicytus ramiflorus)*, whitey-wood, broadleaved forest-edge tree up to 20 metres.

Mānuka: *(Leptospermum scoparium)*, shrub or tree with tiny, sharp aromatic leaves, often conflated with *kānuka*, commonly referred to as tea tree.

Marram: *(Ammophila areneria)*, clumping blue-green perennial grass putting down deep matted roots.

Matipo: *mapou (Myrsine australis)*, small wavy-leaved tree with red stems, grows to 7 metres in forest edge and scrub.

Miro: *(Prumnopitys/Podocarpus ferruginea)*, endemic New Zealand forest conifer up to 25 metres.

Moa: *(Dinornithiformes)*, nine species of now extinct flightless birds endemic to New Zealand. 'Giant Moa' *(Dinornis novaezelandae,* and *D. robustus)* grew to 3.6 metres (12 feet) in height.

Mycelia: (singular: mycelium) long, branching 'threads' grown into spreading masses by fungi above and below ground.

Mynah bird: *(Acridotherestristis).*

Nikau: *(Rhopalostylis sapida)*, a tall native palm tree; its strong fronds on long erect stems were used to construct the walls and/or roofs of traditional dwellings, food stores and for other domestic purposes.

Papatūānuku: Earth Mother/the Land in Māori cosmology; wife of Ranginui, Sun, or Sky Father.

Paradise shelduck: *(Tadorna variegate)*, *putangitangi*, large duck the size and shape of a small goose with a very loud call; endemic to New Zealand.

Pīngao: *(Ficinia spiralis)*, golden sand sedge, native spreading dune grass that holds and binds sand. Culturally important for weaving.

Pittosporum: large genus of tropical shrubs and trees with wide-ranging characteristics of which some twenty-four species are endemic to New Zealand.

Podocarp: trees of the ancient podocarpus genus of tropical evergreen conifers.

Pōhutukawa: *(Metrosideros excelsa)* broadleaved tree to 25 metres with vivid crimson flowers, New Zealand Christmas Tree.

Puka: *(Meryta sinclairii),* evergreen tropical tree to 9 metres with waxy dinner-plate size oval leaves and bunches of black berries. ('*Puka*' may also refer to *Griselinia lucida*, a 5 metre multi-stemmed tree with long, oval glossy leaves.)

Pūkeko: *(Porphyrio melanotus),* endemic swamphen, dark-blue/black wetland bird the size of a chicken, with scarlet beak and forehead, feeds on plants and small animals.

Ponga: (*Cyathea dealbata)* silver fern, tree fern and New Zealand's national symbol. *Ponga* is often used as a common name for other species of tree fern.

Praying mantis: *te whē (Orthodera novaezealandia)* green, long-bodied predatory insect with forelegs adapted to catch and crush its prey.

Pūriri: *(Vitex lucens)* broadleaf evergreen forest tree up to 20 metres, spreading habit, nectar and berries provide year-round food source for birds, endemic to New Zealand.

Ranginui: Sky Father in Māori cosmology; husband of Papatūānuku.

Rengarenga: *(Arthropodium cirratum)*, rock lily, clump-forming perennial plant with broad strap-like leaves and tall spikes of white star-shaped flowers in spring.

Rifleman: *(Acanthisitta chloris)*, New Zealand's smallest bird, tawny-brown with pale breast.

Rimu: *(Dacrydium cupressinum)*, red pine, tropical forest conifer up to 35 metres, juvenile form of long weeping branches, lives up to a thousand years.

Ruru: native owl *(Ninox novaeseelandiae)*, also known as 'more-pork' in mimic of its call.

Shining cuckoo: pīpīwharauroa *(Chrysococcyx lucidus)*, about the size of a sparrow with a metallic bronze-green back and characteristic white and dark-grey horizontal stripes across the front of the body. Females lay a single egg at a time in other species' nests, usually a grey-warbler's.

Swamphen: common name of *pūkeko*.

Taihoa: 'wait a while' *(Cassytha paniculata)*, endemic parasitic scrambling plant of long, tough, leafless strands, producing tiny hermaphrodite flowers.

Tāne: Māori god or *atua* of the forests, progenitor of most flora and fauna.

Tangaroa: Māori god or *atua* of the sea.

Taniwha: shape-shifting spirits, monsters and guardians of sacred places.

Taonga: cultural treasures, including special artefacts and natural species.

Tāwhirimātea: Māori god or *atua* of weather.

Tea tree: common name for both *mānuka* and *kānuka* trees.

Toetoe: *(Cortaderia spp.)*, fountain-shaped clumping grasses from 2 – 6 metres, tall feathery seed heads, differentiated from invasive pampas grass by flowering in spring and summer rather than autumn.

Tōhē: legendary Māori chief who walked and named Te Oneroa-a-Tōhē (The Long Beach of Tōhē) now commonly known as Ninety Mile Beach.

Toheroa: *(Paphies ventricosa)* small clam endemic to New Zealand that breeds in the sea and matures in beach sand.

Tombolo: sand-spit created by migrating dunes that join islands to mainland to form a continuous strip of land.

Tōtara: *(Podocarpus totara)*, 'chief of the forest', forest conifer growing to 30 metres and can live to a thousand years, endemic.

Tuatara: *(Sphenodon punctatus,* and *S. Guntheri)*, extremely rare endemic 'lizards', up to 61 centimetres (24 inches) in length, can live for 100 years, now found only on offshore islands in the Marlborough Sounds.

Tūī: *(Prosthemadera novaeseelandiae)*, forest and garden bird, about the size of a blackbird, black and iridescent green, with two white 'bobbles' of feathers at the throat, sings a range of chuckles, whistles and brief melodies.

Tukutuku: wall panels made from woven dried plant stems and leaves to decorate Māori meeting houses and other special places. They usually depict stories, myths and legends of the weavers' *iwi* or tribe.

Waka: canoe.

Waka-ama: outrigger canoe.

Wattle: common name for various species of Australian *Acacia* trees, freely colonising woodland and scrub in New Zealand and pushing out native species.

Welcome swallow: *(Hirundo neozena),* small member of the swallow family with dark-grey wings and tail, cobalt-blue head and shoulders, red face and throat, and pearly-grey front and under-body. Native to Australia and naturalised in New Zealand since last century.

Wētā: Giant *wētā, pungawētā (Deinacrida heteracantha),* have bodies up to 10 centimetres long, with legs and antennae of the same length; once common, now found only on Little Barrier Island.

Whau: *(Entelea arborescens),* cork tree, endemic evergreen shrub up to 6 metres, with big floppy leaves and sticky-bur seed pods, lives only about 10 years, but self-seeds generously.

White-eye, wax-eye, silvereye, tauhou: *(Zosterops laterallis),* small olive-brown bird, pale-grey breast and edge of wings with a distinctive white band around the eyes. Often flock over berry-bearing bushes and nectar-full flowers, often hanging upside down to reach them.

ANNOTATED LIST OF SPECIES PLANTED ON THE DUNE

Annotated list of native species planted and now established on the Dune, including Māori, common, and scientific names.

Most are species endemic to New Zealand, growing naturally nowhere else; some grow only in Northland, or in only parts of Northland. Most cannot cope with frost, but all tolerate dry, poor soils to varying extents. All are evergreen unless described otherwise, although conifers as well as broadleaf trees shed and renew a proportion of their leaves and needles at intervals.

Estimates of heights are based on trees growing in natural forest; raised outside of their mature forest habitat, native trees rarely reach their full potential height.

FOREST TREES

Griselina, papauma, kapuka, New Zealand mistletoe (*Griselinia littoralis*): a 10-metre tall, multi-stemmed broadleaf tree with thick, glossy green leaves, and small sprays of minute green-white flowers which each produce a single seed. (*Griselinia lucida*, akapuka, is similar but smaller plant with larger leaves and may grow as an epiphyte.) The inner bark was a traditional medicine for skin ailments. Thick waxy leaves help trees to reduce evaporation and retain moisture; several of both species thrive on the Dune and were unaffected by the recent drought.

Horoeka, lancewood (*Pseudopanax crassifolius*): in maturity, a 15-metre tree with a crown of thick serrated leaves. It is better known for its extraordinary juvenile form which lasts for 20 years: from the top of a thin unbranched trunk sculptured with longitudinal ridges and hollows, emerge long, very narrow, deeply serrated leaves, often with a prominent dark-red or pinkish midrib. *Pseudopanax ferox* is similar though smaller (to about 5 metres), but its leaves are darker and longer, to 50 cm (18 inches) and serrations deeper, ending in tiny spikes that can puncture the skin. Slow to grow on the Dune but persevering.

Kahikatea, white pine, (*Dacrycarpus dacrydioides*): conifer of the ancient Podocarpus genus dating to at least 160 million years ago. Can grow to 50+ metres and live 600 years or more. Hermaphrodite (monoecious), i. e. male and female cones are borne on the same plant. Sweet red berries were a traditional food source; hazardous to collect as mature trees shed their lateral branches leaving a tall clean bole. A group of three, planted in a fairly damp corner at the base of the Dune, grew quickly without any setbacks; the tallest is now about 10 metres.

Karaka (*Corynocarpus laevigatus*): broadleaf tree growing to about 16 metres, bearing thick glossy dark-green leaves, and tiny, white, hermaphrodite flowers. The large orange fruits were an important food source for Māori. The seed kernel – rich in protein – contains the toxin *karakin,* which was removed by steaming in earth ovens for several days. The cooked nuts could then be stored for a year or more. Karaka struggle on the dry slopes of the Dune, but although their growth is stunted, they have fruited and freely self-sown.

Kauri (*Agathis australis*): New Zealand's iconic tree, symbolic of Tane, god of the forest and all its creatures, grows naturally only in Northland beyond 38 degrees of latitude. Conifers of the ancient Araucaria family, kauri remain in juvenile form for up to 30 years; grow to over 50 metres; and can live for 4,000 years. The Greek 'agathis', means 'a ball of string', describing the round, green female cones the size of a golf ball; male cones look like miniature cigars. Highly prized for resin and timber, the few remaining forests are now protected. Of twelve kauri planted in three different locations on the

Dune, seven died in the recent severe drought, but the five longest established trees (planted 15–20 years ago) appear to have survived, though the effects of drought can be long-term.

Kawaka (*Libocedrus plumosa*, literally 'fragrant cedar'): lowland forest conifer with a restricted natural distribution mainly in Northland, growing to 25 metres but extremely slowly. Branchlets, thickly lined with dark-green flattened leaves, have a feathery look. Branch tips produce both male and female cones, the latter containing winged seeds. All three kawaka on the Dune have grown strongly, withstood the drought, and are producing cones.

Kohekohe (*Dysoxylum spectabile*): broadleaf coastal tree growing to 15 metres, like many tropical trees, it is cauliflory, i. e. its long panicles of small, waxy, white flowers emerge straight out of the bark of its trunk and branches. In traditional medicine, a decoction of bark and the soft bright-green leaves were consumed as a tonic. The three trees planted on the Dune were slow to grow initially, but are now established and flowering.

Kōwhai *(Sophora microphylla):* the small-leafed species of this spectacular tree that can grow to 25 metres (*S. tetraptera*, a larger-leaved species, grows to 10 metres), and both produces hanging racemes of bright yellow flowers that look like a golden crown in spring, and develops dangling chains of wood-hard seed casings in summer. Kōwhai is one of New Zealand's few deciduous or semi-deciduous trees; the flowers on two of those on the Dune often precede new leaves. Long drooping leaf stems bearing tiny leaflets give the tree a feathering appearance. Native wood pigeons and bell birds are especially fond of the flowers and seeds, and *tūi* birds love the nectar. The inner bark was used in traditional medicine to cure skin itches caused by parasites.

Lancewood – see Horoeka

Maire, maire rauriki, white maire (*Nestegis lanceolata*): lowland forest tree producing long, narrow tawny-brown leaves and racemes of tiny pale-green flowers without petals. Maire can grow to 15 metres, but those on the dune have struggled to establish and were further set back by the drought. Traditionally, its hard wood was used to make clubs and spears.

Matai, black pine, (*Prumnopitys taxifolia*): ancient conifer species growing to 25 metres or more and living for a thousand years. Traditionally, the wood was used for carving implements and food bowls, and for brown dye. Matai is slow to mature – the first specimen planted on the Dune still bears its tangled bronze juvenile form and has gained little more than a metre in 10 years, but it survived the drought without visible damage. New growth – tiny, lime green needles – stand out in contrast as they emerge from the wiry orange stems.

Milkwood, ewekuri, pukariao (*Streblus banksii*): named for its white sap which early European settlers used as a milk substitute; a coastal, lowland forest tree growing to about 12 metres – uncommon in many areas. On male trees, where mid-green oval leaves join stems, long spikes of massed, minute green flowers dangle down for 5 cm; on female trees, the spikes of sparse flowers are much shorter and stick up, hanging down only later with the weight of tiny red fruit.

Miro, brown pine, (*Prumnopitys ferruginea*): ancient conifer of lowland forest growing to 25 metres and living at least 600 years. The resinous bark produces a brown dye, but also has many medicinal uses: to treat ulcers and wounds; and infused with the lime-green needle-leaves to treat gastric ailments and gonorrhoea (*paipai*). Extremely slow growing, especially in the challenging conditions of the Dune, but those planted on the cooler south-facing slope survived the drought unscathed. The main stem of one on the north-facing slope died back completely, but a long lateral branch from near the base is growing to replace it.

Pigeonwood, porokaiwhiri (*Hedycarya arborea*): lowland and montane forest tree to 12 metres with dark-green oval leaves and tiny white flowers. Copious green berries, bright-red when ripe, are a favourite with kererū (kūkupa), the native wood pigeon whose eating habits make it a prolific planter of native trees. Leaves are believed to have been used for vapour baths. Pigeonwood is found throughout the length of New Zealand and is flourishing on the Dune, and already producing bird-sown saplings.

Pōhutukawa (*Metrosideros excelsa*): nick-named New Zealand's Christmas tree because of the vivid crimson (sometimes yellow), hermaphrodite, brush-like flowers that cover the tree in December. A broadleaf coastal tree with thick, dark- to olive-green leaves, velvety with a thick whitish tomentum on their undersides, pōhutukawa can grow to 20 metres and live for 800 years. Traditionally, nectar was gathered from its flowers as a sweetener, and its hard wood (the Greek, *metrosideros,* means 'heart of iron') was employed to make canoe thwarts. But pōhutukawa's main cultural significance is its mythological role in the final journey of the spirits of the dead. I planted more than twenty pōhutukawa in various locations all over the Dune, and though rates of growth have differed according to soil moisture and exposure, all survived the drought with the help of the tomentum on their leaves which reduces water loss by evaporation. A few more have been planted to replace other species that died.

Pukatea (*Laurelia novae-zelandiae)*: a slim, lowland tree growing to 35 metres, hermaphrodite flowers and thick, bottle-green oval leaves, edged with smooth shallow serrations. In very young plants, the stems are deep mahogany red; in maturity, the bark is silvery, and the base of the trunk is dramatically buttressed.

Pukatea prefers damp conditions but I planted one on the Dune recently to extend diversity and because it is a pretty tree. It is in a place where it can receive watering support when needed. Traditionally, the timber was used to carve figureheads of canoes; medicinally, a decoction of the inner bark was a treatment for skin ailments and toothache.

Pūriri (*Vitex lucens*), a broadleaf tree with bright-green wavy-crinkly leaves, pūriri grows to about 20 metres. The hermaphrodite, small cerise flowers and bright-red berries provide nectar and fruit for *tūi* and other birds throughout the year. The twelve pūriri planted on the Dune have grown at different rates, the best growth in locations with more natural moisture and nutrients, but none succumbed to the drought. Seeds germinate readily and are being raised for further plantings.

Rewarewa, New Zealand honeysuckle, (*Knightia excelsa*): 30-metre tall tree of lowland forests, with long, narrow, thick, serrated leaves of tawny-green; rewarewa not only tolerates but needs dry, poor soils – it may die if fed with nutrients. Long racemes of tightly packed, gorgeous blood-red flowers with dramatically curling petals provide nectar for birds; the chocolate-brown velvety seed pods, when emptied of their pair of winged seeds, look like tiny canoes. The inner bark of rewarewa was used to stem bleeding and heal wounds; the timber is carved into craft items. All except one of the seven trees planted on the Dune in dry, exposed places rode through the drought without damage. The one that died was the most recently planted (about 8 years ago). A few more have been planted on both north- and south-facing slopes.

Rimu, red pine (*Dacrydium cupressinum*): another ancient conifer species that grows to 35 metres and may live to almost 1,000 years. Slender weeping branches that trail to the ground in juveniles are replaced by a bare lower trunk and shorter leaves in maturity. Male and female fruits and cones are usually found on separate trees (i e. dioecious). Infusions of bark were a traditional remedy for skin sores, ulcers and burns. All five specimens on the Dune withstood the drought with a minimum of die-back on some branches.

Tanekaha, celery pine, *(Phyllocladus trichomanoides)*: a tough conifer that grows to 25 metres and may live for 500 years. Long drooping branches are covered in pale yellowish-green flattened leaflets giving a doily appearance. Bark is used to produce dark-red and musky-pink dyes for weaving. All three specimens planted on the Dune coped with the drought with no apparent ill effects.

Tarata, lemonwood (*Pittosporum eugenioides*): a 12-metre lowland forest tree, with silvery-grey trunk and branches; undulating, light-olive-green leaves, and pale-yellow sweetly fragranced flowers. Tarata have grown more slowly than expected on the Dune and suffered several episodes of die-back; they struggle in dry periods because their leaves are thin and without tormentum, but they endure.

Tawapu (*Pouteria costata, previously Planchonella novozelandica*): a broadleaf tree with small, thick glossy dark-green leaves, whose stems and branches bleed a white sap when cut. Tawapu is not common, its distribution restricted to headlands and rocky islands off the north-east coast of Northland where it grows to about 15 metres. The one specimen planted at the top of the Dune twelve years ago is 3 metres tall and has not yet produced its tiny white flowers and deep red fruits, but it survived the drought with daily watering; an effort extended because of its relative rarity.

Titoki (*Alectryon excelsus spp. excelsus*): a pretty, broadleaf coastal tree growing to 10 metres; its sets of seven light-green leaflets give a feathery appearance at a distance. Tiny hermaphrodite flowers bear no petals, and produce bright-red fruit which are poisonous but eaten when cooked. Crushed leaves were a traditional treatment for insect bites. Of the three trees on the Dune, two coped well with the drought; the one on the dryer north-facing slope died after putting up a good fight by trying to maintain some lower branches.

Toro (*Myrsine salicina*): 10-metre tall, tough lowland broadleaf, with long, narrow, olive-green leathery leaves with rounded tips. Tiny white or pink flowers emerge straight from the branches. Two toro seedlings planted eight years on a dry, exposed location, though extremely slow to grow, have both survived the drought without any attention; several others have since been planted in various locations to replace some of the lost kauri.

Toru (*Toronia toru, previously Persoonia toru*): a member of the *Protea* family, long, narrow shiny leaves, with pointed tips are yellow-green with occasional red tips or markings, or even a whole red leaf. It grows naturally only in Northland lowland forests and scrub, and can reach more than 10 metres. A single specimen was planted as a seedling on the Dune; it has grown extremely slowly and needed supplementary watering throughout the summer.

Tōtara, 'chief of the forest' (*Podocarpus totara var. totara*): ancient hermaphrodite conifer species with yellowish-green needles that darken with age, grows to 30 metres or more, and lives for about 1,000 years. The subject of many Māori stories and proverbs around strength and leadership, tōtara's timber is highly valued for making canoes because its resin resists rot. The tree's natural oil – totarol – contains important anti-bacterial properties currently being tested on antibiotic-resistant infections. All ten saplings planted on the Dune have grown well without any attention and remain vigorous; the tallest about 8 metres so far.

FOREST EDGE, WOODLAND AND
OPEN GROUND TREES:

Most are smaller trees below 8 metres and are among the toughest species, often being the first tree pioneers in clearings and open scrub exposed by fire. All are evergreen.

Akeake (*Dodonaea viscosa*): narrowly oval, thin, almost crisp leaves and open growth habit of akeake make it a useful nurse tree to shade and shelter other saplings. It is fast growing and self-seeds readily from a profusion of winged seeds that develop from tiny green-white flowers without petals. Akeake means 'forever and ever', describing the wood that is extremely hard and strong, and used to make clubs, spears and staves. Pale-green and dark-red varieties each produce matching seeds. Akeake flourishes so well on the Dune that it sometimes has to be weeded out where it has seeded too profusely for the welfare of its neighbours.

Daisy tree, akiraho, golden akeake (*Olearia paniculata*), and tanguru (*O. Albida var. angulata*): two of over 100 species of *Olearia* endemic to New Zealand. Both grow to between 4 to 6 metres depending on conditions, and bear distinctively tough wavy leaves – yellowish-green on akiraho, olive-green on tanguru – with a white tomentum on the underside which helps to retain moisture. Stems of small white hermaphrodite flowers produce tufted seeds like tiny paint brushes. On the Dune, both have grown well though slowly. Tanguru occurs naturally only on the Aupōuri Peninsular and East Cape, and as it is threatened in the wild and difficult to source commercially, cuttings and seeds are being propagated for future plantings.

Cabbage tree (*Cordyline species*): see ti kouka.

Five-finger (*Pseudopanax species*): see Houpara.

Horopito, pepper tree (*Pseudowintera axillaris*): thin, glossy, slightly wavy pale- to sage-green leaves on red stems, with occasional smudgy red markings or red edges on leaves. Groups of tiny green-white flowers emerge from the bark of branches and develop into bright red berries. When crushed, the leaves smell peppery and dried leaves are used as a spice in cooking. An infusion of the bitter-tasting outer bark is recorded as a substitute for quinine in traditional medicine. Two of the smaller, shrub species, *Pseudowintera colorata* with red-margined and red-blotched leaves, perished after a few years on the Dune. The *P. axillaris* grows up to 8 metres and has continued slow but healthy growth.

Houpara, whauwhaupaku, five-finger (*Pseudopanax lessonii*): dark-green, thick glossy and deeply veined composite leaves forming 'hands' of three to five 'fingers' or leaflets. Tiny white, pink or dark red flowers produce massed green berries, black when ripe and much sought after by birds. Not a good nurse tree with its wide crown and dense growth, but they are relatively fast growing, their bird-borne seeds germinate readily, and they flourish all over the Dune. The name 'five-finger' is commonly given to several *Pseudopanax* species with composite leaves which may be divided into as many as seven 'fingers'; their flowers may be pink or white.

Kānuka (*Kunzia erocoides*): see Tea tree

Karo (*Pittosporum crassifolium*): tough pioneer tree with olive-green, leathery and slightly wavy leaves. New leaves and buds are felted with a white tomentum, giving an attractive background to clusters of small, fragrant, deep-red to burgundy flowers, and sticky black seeds that germinate readily – so prolifically that seedlings in the wrong places on the Dune have to be weeded out. Karo can grow to 10 metres though usually less, and its open growth habit makes it a useful nurse tree.

Kawakawa, pepper tree (not to be confused with horopito which is also commonly referred to as 'pepper tree'), (*Macropiper excelsum)*: a shade-loving small tree to about 6 metres, with distinctive bright-green heart-shaped leaves on black stems much jointed at all angles. The soft, thin leaves are prey to caterpillars. Spikes of cream-coloured fruits, orange when ripe, stand upright like narrow candles. Kawakawa is a culturally important plant and every part of it has medicinal or ritual uses (further details in the main text, page 139).

Kiekie (*Freycinetia banksii*): a scrambling shrub with long (1.5 metres), narrow, almost grass-like dark-green leaves sprouting out from along thin stems and branches, kiekie spreads along the ground, leans on trees for support, or climbs them with its aerial roots. On separate male and female plants, flowers emerge in fleshy bracts of cream or mauve-pink; female flowers are pale pinkish-brown, the mature fruit dark brown, knobbly and sausage-shaped. The cigar-shaped male flowers are paler and thinner. Several kiekie flourish in the damp semi-shade at the base of the south slope and are already using their aerial roots to entwine and climb small trees.

Kohuhu (*Pittosporum tenuifolium*): one of some twenty-four species of *Pittosporum* endemic to New Zealand, Kohuhu grows to 8 metres. Mid-green slightly wavy leaves, and small very dark red, sweet-smelling flowers grow from smooth, almost black stems and trunk. Kohuhu is one of several aromatic species whose leaves were steamed in traditional vapour baths. They suffered die-back during drought but seem to recover when conditions become more favourable. *Pittosporum* species are a popular garden tree in New Zealand and many commercial hybrids are available.

Mahoe, whitey-wood *(Melicytus ramiflorus)*: although mahoe can grow to 10 metres, it has a spreading habit, often dividing into branches from near ground level and prefers more open conditions along the forest edge.

Longish oval leaves of tawny-green are lightly toothed; tiny yellowish flowers and purple berries (sometimes used to make dyes) emerge from branch stems.

Lacebark, houhere (*Hoheria populnea*): named for the tissue-like white fibre of its inner bark used in traditional weaving, houhere is a coastal lowland tree growing to 8 metres, and produces masses of small white, star-shaped flowers and winged seeds. Soft, mid-green leaves are serrated; in *H. Populnea purpurea*, the undersides of leaves are purple, the veins more prominently so. Those planted on the flat below the south slope are growing well.

Makamaka *(Ackama rosifolia):* a pretty tree with a spreading habit. Long leaf-stems (petioles) bear oval serrated leaflets of lime-green when new, darkening when older, with prominent red veins in their undersides; in a breeze, they resemble green and red feathers. Sprays of minute cream-coloured flowers emerge from branch tips giving a frothy appearance in spring. Makamaka was marginally suitable for planting on the Dune; it would prefer more moisture and better soil than is available. One died during the severe drought and will not be replaced, three others experienced severe die-back but seem to be recovering.

Makomako, wineberry (*Aristotelia serrata*): a spreading tree with soft, serrated tawny-brown leaves on thin branches, from which sprays of mixed pink, cream and red flowers emerge from the bark and develop into small black berries; a good source of bird food. Makomako would prefer more moisture and better soil than is available on the Dune; up to the present, they are surviving rather than thriving.

Mānuka (*Leptospermum scoparium*): see Tea Tree

Matipo, red matipo, mapou (*Myrsine australis*): a vigorous, tough pioneering small tree with thin, silver-grey bark (darkening with age) and yellowy-green wavy leaves on red stems; the leaves edged and blotched in red. Tiny cream-coloured flowers emerge along the stems and develop black seeds. It self-seeds readily and also sends up new stems from roots up to a metre from the parent tree. One two-metre matipou in a particularly dry place appeared to die completely during the drought, but after a few weeks of rain, new shoots are growing out from the trunk near its base. Those elsewhere on the Dune are flourishing. Matipo has ceremonial importance in traditional Māori culture and was used also in making adze shafts.

Mingimingi (*Leucopogon fasciculatus*) (not to be confused with *Coprosma propinqua* which is sometimes referred to as mingimingi): small vigorous tree to 5 metres, with rough, brown-grey figured bark, and masses of small, pointed blue-green leaves. Racemes of minute white flowers hang from branch tips, and later bear tiny red berries. Mingimingi grows profusely, seeds readily, and is a valuable pioneer, stabilising soil and sheltering other tree seedlings.

Ngaio, kaio (*Myoporum laetum*): coastal lowland tree occasionally to 10 metres, spreading habit, wind and salt resistant, but they have been slow to grow on the Dune and experience a lot of die-back. Ngaio produces tiny white, red-speckled flowers and red-purple berries. Both the berries and the grey-green oval leaves (their undersides covered in oil glands) are poisonous to humans and livestock, but the oils (mannitol and ngaione) have medicinal qualities: a poultice of crushed leaves was used traditionally to draw boils and heal wounds, and a decoction of fresh leaves was applied to the scalp to clear dandruff.

Parapara *(Pisonia brunoniana)*: small (to 6 metres) broadleaf tree with large dark-green glossy leaves. It grows naturally only in the northern coastal fringe and outer islands. Parapara is known as the 'bird-catcher' tree because its large racemes of seedpods are extremely sticky and may trap birds to their death. Only one specimen is planted on the Dune, a variegated cultivar because, apparently, they are less effective in trapping birds. The naturalist friend checking the text took me to task for this sentiment, commenting: 'All part of the ecosystem. Rotting birds feed the roots.' I accept the scolding but remain unreformed.

Tawhiri karo (*Pittosporum cornifolium*): grows to 2 metres (though the specimen on the Dune is planted in the ground, it usually grows as an epiphyte in native forest), with mid-green, pointed, oval leaves and small pinky-brown, star-shaped flowers with long narrow petals. Small green seed capsules open to reveal a surprising bright red interior and a group of black shiny seeds.

Tea tree: common name applied informally to both mānuka (*Leptospermum scoparium*) and kānuka (*Kunzia ericoides*), and both are members of the Myrtle family. Some six subspecies of kānuka and two unnamed forms of mānuka range in size from prostrate shrubs to 8-metre trees. The tree forms share the same general appearance of rough, often gnarled or wrinkled grey-brown bark, and tawny-green foliage ranging in nature from soft thin needles (kānuka), to small narrow leaves shaped like tiny lance blades (mānuka) covering long wispy stems Small individual flowers emerge along the stems in spring, generally white, but also occasionally pink (selective breeding by horticulturists has produced a range of pink and red cultivars). Both mānuka and kānuka grow in similar habitats and, depending on their size, provide sources of medicinal oils, food for birds and insects (e. g. nectar for mānuka honey), fuel, wind-breaks, and timber for building and tools. A pioneer species with wide tolerance of growing conditions, their roots stabilise sandy soils and their open structure provides light shade for young plants which makes them good 'nursery trees'. Tea tree grow readily from seed, and by scattering seed-bearing trimmings and branches on the ground as mulch. They are stars on the Dune.

Tī kōuka, cabbage tree (*Cordyline species*): thin, clean but crinkled-looking trunks, branched in some species, are topped by dense tufts of long narrow leaves and large panicles of tiny white fragrant flowers producing white or black berries (depending on species). The crown centre, the 'cabbage', was a traditional source of food, along with the roots, and leaves were used for weaving and rope-making. Of the large number of tī kōuka planted in various locations on the Dune, few survived the first few years and these continue to struggle. The ground everywhere is too dry for them and no more will be planted.

Tī koraha or tī rauriki, dwarf cabbage tree (*Cordyline pumilio*): clumps of long narrow leaves grow like a fountain from ground level; in maturity, growing to one metre tall on short (30 centimetre) smooth trunks. A group of *pumilio* (a red-leaved cultivar) planted on the Dune's south slope have fared better than their full-sized cousins, and produce long sprays of tiny, delicate, widely-spaced whitish-pink flowers.

Wharangi, waioriki (*Melicope ternata*): a sturdy coastal small tree, or a multi-stemmed shrub when growing in open ground. From the stems between the sets of three smooth, shiny, pale-green leaves, tiny white, green-tinged flowers emerge on short stems also in sets of three; bunches of brown seed pods open to reveal a trio of black shiny seeds (the Latin '*ternus*' means 'in threes). Wharangi produce small amounts of aromatic gum used traditionally to sweeten bad breath. They flourish in various sites all over the Dune.

Whau, cork tree (*Entelea arboresens*): a fast-growing small tree to about 6 metres, endemic to the northern part of Northland. Whau is characterised by very large, floppy, slightly serrated mid-green leaves, white flowers, and large dark-brown spiky seed capsules like burrs. The wood is much lighter than balsa-wood and was used for making fish-net floats and rafts. Whau lives only about 10 years but self seeds readily: the third generation of a tree planted on a favoured part of the Dune is already mature.

SHRUBS AND CLIMBERS

The understorey of native forest wherever sufficient light penetrates; and pioneer species who prefer open ground.

Alseuosmia macrophylla, toropapa: large multi-stemmed shrub to 5 metres, pale green elongated leaves, slightly serrated, and small red hermaphrodite flowers. As the name suggests – 'alseuosmia' derives from the Greek, 'pleasant fragrance of the grove' – the shrub gives off a strong sweet-spice fragrance.

Corokia buddleioides, korokio taranga, korokoro: endemic lowland 3-metre shrub with lance-shaped mid-green and brown-edged glossy leaves, dark bark, sprays of tiny yellow flowers and dark-red to black berries; it grows well even on the dryer north-facing slope of the Dune. Traditionally, young shoots were chewed to relieve dysentery and stomach ache.

Corokia cotoneaster: 3-metre shrub of wiry tangled stems with tiny oval leaves, yellow flowers and red or yellow fruit. Plants have been slow to establish and still struggle in dry periods.

Corokia cultivars: a large number of cultivars have been developed, selected for berry colours of yellow, red, orange, maroon, and leaves ranging from bright glossy green to variegated green/brown to cream/yellow; all have flourished on the Dune and have proved among the toughest shrubs to cope with drought, while providing an excellent source of bird food.

Coprosma spp., a genus of over 100 species of shrubs ranging from small trees to sprawling ground covers, and with an unfortunate name: from the Greek 'kopros' (dung) and 'osme' (odour). Leaves vary from smooth round-edged to needle-like and vary in size, thickness and glossiness, but flowers are similar: tiny white-green with minute petals and long dangling stamens to aid wind pollination. The following species are all growing on the Dune, less well on the driest sites where karamu suffered the most die-back during the drought: *C. grandifolia*, kanono; *C. macrocarpa*, karamu; *C. lucida*, shining karamu; *C. repens*, taupata; *C. parviflora; C. acerosa,* needle-leafed, ground-hugging sand-coprosma; and an unidentified tiny-round-leafed bushy coprosma that has spread naturally throughout the Dune, providing a useful understorey.

Hangehange, New Zealand privet (*Geniostoma rupestre var. ligustrifolium*): multi-stemmed bushy shrub with bright-green oval pointed leaves. The turned-down petals of tiny cream-white flowers are covered in hairs (*geniostoma* means 'hairy throat'), and are intensely fragrant with a musk-spicy scent similar to turmeric. Infusions were used in traditional medicine to ease itchy skin conditions. The two planted specimens experienced severe die-back during the recent severe drought but have since rallied. Cuttings have been taken to grow and plant in more favourable positions, especially desirable to maintain as hangehange is associated with kauri forests.

Hebe spp.: of the 100 species in New Zealand ranging in habit from prostrate to 7-metre shrubs, the tall, narrow-leaved species endemic to the Far North and listed here has survived better than others that were tried. Their narrow leaves help to slow evaporation during dry periods, but they are sensitive to severe drought: *Hebe stricta,* koromiko (the leaves an important traditional medicine for dysentery); *H. parviflora*, koromiko taranga; and *H. macrocarpa*, kokomuka.

Hibiscus trionum, puarangi: annual or biannual herb to 40 cm; stems covered in stiff hairs and bearing large, paper-thin white flower petals with maroon centres.

They self germinate readily, maintaining an almost permanent presence in open sunny positions.

Lophomyrtus bullata, ramarama: the Latin '*bulla*' means 'bubble' – my nick-name for ramarama is 'bubble-wrap bush': a small tree to about 6 metres, its natural distribution confined mostly to Northland, with small, oval, puckered glossy leaves, mid-green blotched haphazardly with cream, pink, brown and red. Tiny, white, hermaphrodite flowers produce dark-red to black berries.

Marlborough Rock Daisy, *Pachystegia insignis*: indigenous l-metre spreading shrub whose natural occurrence is limited to only Eastern Marlborough and North Canterbury in South Island, but its oval, thick leathery leaves with furry tomentum on stems and leaves adapts it to dry rocky habitats, and its hermaphrodite, large daisy-like flowers are attractive, so I tried 3 plants on the Dune. They have survived drought, but after several years, remain ground-hugging and produce only 1 or 2 flowers each year – it is probably too hot and humid for them to flourish.

Muehlenbeckia axillaris: ground-hugging scrambler whose thin dark wiry stems bearing tiny dark-green leaves can form a dense mat, but strands can also scramble up and through small shrubs. Well adapted to poor dry soils, it is spreading cautiously.

Pomaderris spp.: woody shrubs to 7 metres with clusters of cream-beige hermaphrodite flowers. The following main species flourish on the Dune providing ground-cover and stabilising sandy slopes: *P. apetala*, tainui, dark green leaves longer than other species are narrow and wrinkled, tiny beige flowers spaced out along long racemes, dense growth can spread over several metres; *P. kumeraho*, kumarahou, upright shrub to 3 metres, leaves oval, smooth and mid-green, and dense clusters of tiny cream flowers at the tips of branches; *P. phylicifolia*, low-growing shrub with short, pointed, almost needle-like, dark green leaves and small clusters of tiny beige flowers emerging from leaf axils. Of these, only kumarahou is important in traditional medicine – infusions of leaves are still commonly used to ease respiratory and kidney ailments.

Rhabdothamnus solandri, taurepo, New Zealand gloxinia: slender branching shrub to about 2 metres bearing round, serrated moss-green leaves covered in short stiff brown hairs, and delicate short tubular flowers that hang down like tiny orange bells. Natural distribution is confined to Northland forest. Two shrubs on the Dune established slowly in poor dry soils, but are managing to grow in the dappled light of a light canopy. One of the many shrubs whose leaves were used in making vapour baths in traditional medicine.

Rata vine, akatea, white rata, (*Metrosideros perforata*), and akatawhiwhi, red rata (*M. fulgens*): ground-scrambling much-branching lianas with thin dark stems, tiny leathery dark-green leaves, and small brush-like hermaphrodite flowers in white, and red respectively (leaves and flowers are considerably larger in red rata). Both are covering ground on the Dune's south-facing slope and successfully progressing up tree trunks (they are not parasitic and do no harm to their host). Two variegated cream-green cultivars are also flourishing.

Solanum laciniatum, poroporo, nightshade: fast-growing, branching woody shrub to about 3 metres, long pointed dark-green leaves of irregular shape, flowers of thin purple petals and large oval fruits, orange when ripe (poisonous when green). An open habit gives it a spindly appearance. Poroporo grew well as a pioneer shrub on open sunny sites, and has disappeared naturally as planted trees and shrubs create shade and competition.

Supple jack, kareao (*Ripogonum scandens*): branching liana with lance-shaped dark green leaves on a thick strong main stem that can climb to 8 metres; used traditionally for multiple medical applications, their scarlet berries and young shoots were also eaten. Stems were used to weave fish traps, coarse baskets, to lash fences and in general construction. One specimen, planted early in the project below the south slope, appeared to die out, but has since re-grown and is flourishing.

Tecomanthe speciosa: endemic vine with thick woody stems extending to 10 metres, bearing dark-green, glossy elongated oval leaves. Dramatic, long, white, waxy trumpet flowers cluster in groups of up to 30 on a single stem, each opening in turn. The long brown hard seed pods may contain as many as 200 winged seeds. Only one plant remains growing in the wild, on Three Kings Islands – the story of the species' rescue is told in Chapter 5.

GRASSES AND GROUND COVERS

Astelia spp.: kakaha, 'silver spear' (*Astelia chathamica)*, named for its long gracefully curved leaves glowing with a silvery sheen; kowharawhara, tree *Astelia* (*A. Solandri)*, an epiphyte in the wild and grown in the crux of a tree on the Dune; wharawhara (*A.banksii)*, long narrow silver-green leaves. *Astelia* bear racemes of tiny silvery-green flowers from their centres; female plants produce black or red fruits depending on species; 'kauri grass' (*A. trinervia),* an associate of the natural kauri forests of Northland. The stiff narrow grass-like leaves of this *Astelia* can grow to 2 metres, but the dryness of the Dune has challenged them: the surviving plants are no more than 50 cm high.

Brachyglottis greyi: a 2-metre straggly shrub bearing oval olive-green leaves with white felt tomentum on their undersides and stems, which adapt it to dry conditions by reducing evaporation. The daisy-like flowers are buttercup yellow; when the mass of tiny winged seeds develop from the centre, they look like miniature powder-puffs. The natural distribution of this species of *Brachyglottis* is the southern end of North Island, not the Far North, and although one specimen continues to grow and flower on the Dune, it has not flourished and no more have been planted.

Cutty grass, mapere (*Gahnia setifolia*): also called 'razor sedge' for good reason: the razor-sharp edges of its long drooping dark-green blades can cut deep into the flesh. It has naturally colonised most parts of the Dune from wind-borne seeds, or those preserved in the soil and germinating after the disturbance of weeding or planting, but small plants in the wrong place are gathered and grown-on for transplanting into loose sandy patches that need to be stabilised. Cutty grass has deep, fibrous, tenacious roots, and large clumps make a good hand-hold when clambering around the slopes – provided one is wearing sturdy gloves.

Carex testacaea: a clumping sedge with long, thread-like arching stems ending in seed heads like tiny barley heads. Stems begin green, but grown in full sun they take on brilliant copper tones. Of all the species of clumping native grasses and sedges tried on the Dune, this one is the star; it sometimes grows smaller than its full potential of 45 cm, but nonetheless flourishes in the dry poor soils, withstands drought, and self-seeds and transplants readily.

Chionochloa flavicans: a clumping grass of 1-2 metre long, with green weeping leaves and arching flower stalks that overtop the clump with pale creamy-green feathery seed heads. Its natural occurrence is limited to Northland.

Cortaderia toetoe renamed *C. austroderia*: toetoe (toitoi): tall native grass forming fountains of greenish-blue leaves, toetoe grows up to 2 metres tall; slightly arching stems bear large feathery-gold seed heads (smaller and more elegant than the invasive exotic 'pampas grass' that can push toetoe out of its natural habitat). Toetoe has many important uses in Māori traditions, including weaving and ritual. Other native *Cortaderia* species with differences in size and colour tones also bear the common name toetoe: *C. fulvida; C. splendens; C. richardii.*

Dianella nigra, native blueberry (though the berries, ranging in colour from pale blue to indigo, are tiny): a clumping plant with long mid-green leaves, often reddish at the base, and much narrower and softer than flax. They cope well with dry poor soils and many have self-sown, helping to stabilise steep banks.

Flax: see *Phormiun spp.*

Libertia peregrinans, native iris: stiff, flat green and orange striped leaves grow to 40 cm in a fan formation, and spread by underground rhizomes as well as seed from the small white flowers atop long orange stalks; a dry-tolerant groundcover often growing naturally among sand dunes, *Libertia* is slowly establishing along sunny edges of paths.

Machaerina sinclairii, tūhara: clump-forming sedge with smooth strap-like shiny-green leaves, topped by arching stems of bright tan seed heads; a tough plant doing well at the bottom of the cooler south-facing slope.

Phormiun spp., flax: harakeke (*P. tenax*): the larger species, whose wide moss-green blades stand erect up to 3 metres, supported by prominent pale mid-ribs. Strong, rigid, flowering stems stand higher above the clump like a banner held aloft, bearing bright burnt-orange to red funnel flowers, which will later form elongated pods of black shiny flat seeds. Wharariki, mountain flax – though not restricted to mountains (*P. cookianum*), bears shorter strap leaves to 2 metres, less stiff and in a brighter green; its golden yellow flowers bear long red stamens. Over 100 flax plants of both species have been planted on the Dune to hold soil on the slopes, and provide nectar and seed sources for birds. Tolerant of a wide range of conditions, they all flourish and planting continues. But harakeke also has significant cultural importance for traditional weaving, rope making, medicine, food from the fleshy root tuber, and ritual. Dozens of cultivars of varying colours, sizes and habit are commercially available, but they tend to be less tolerant and need more care and water; they have not thrived on the Dune.

Pimelia prostrata, New Zealand Daphne: the blue-green tiny-leaved stems ending in tinier white flowers initially flourished, draping and spreading over cooler south-facing banks, but have gradually receded and are now absent as a result of increasing dryness.

Rengarenga, rock lily (*Arthropodium cirratum*): a clumping perennial, whose soft, bright green leaves as wide but much shorter than flax (about 50 cm), drape gracefully from the centre, their tips coming to a sudden, elongated point. Flower stalks rise for up to a metre above the clump, each producing multiple small white star-shaped flowers with long, vivid yellow stamens that hang down over the plant. Rengarenga's tolerance allows it to grow well as a ground-cover in multiple sites on the Dune.

Toetoe: see *Cortadaria toetoe.*

Xeronema callistemon, Poor Knight's Lily, a clumping perennial, bearing fans of smooth bright-green strap-like leaves up to a metre long; slightly longer flower stems lean out over the leaves, the end third of their length opening into tight rows of bright crimson flowers, each like the bristles of a tiny brush – the overall effect gave it the nick-name 'the toothbrush plant'. It occurs naturally only in Poor Knight's and Hen and Chicken Islands; slow growing, irregularly flowering, and preferring richer soil, only two are planted near the cottage as features of interest and occasional excitement when a flower stalk is clearly developing.

FERNS

With the exception of the dry fern, *Doodia*, which has spread naturally over large areas of the Dune's surface, ferns are generally problematic on the Dune to varying degrees; most have been selected for tolerance to dryness and planted in carefully selected shady sites, but a few less tolerant species are supported by watering throughout summer to maintain diversity of vegetation, and for my own pleasure. How many will continue into a drier future is uncertain.

Adiatum hispidulum, rosy maidenhair fern: wiry black stipes or stems bear up to seven deep olive-green fronds, splayed out fanwise, each varying in length up to 30 cm. Young fronds emerge pink-tinged. In time, the stipes branch and a dense mass forms. Three small patches have established themselves on the Dune where the tree canopy has created shady sites.

Asplenium bulbiferum, chicken and hen fern: a ground fern with wide, gracefully drooping lacy fronds of light green that can reach 1 metre in height; it is tougher than most and generally survive without watering. Tiny miniature ferns develop from frond tips and may take root when they drop, and new shoots will often emerge from the ground after a plant appears to have died.

Blechnum fraseri, maukurangi: miniature tree ferns growing to about a metre tall; adapted to dry Northland forest, but even in the specially shaded patch where they were planted they need summer watering on the fast-draining sand of the Dune. Plants develop dense colonies by pushing up new shoots from creeping rhizomes and their number has already tripled.

Blechnum spp.: one specimen each of the following ferns were planted in a small shaded area at the top of the Dune accessible to watering: piupiu, crown fern *(B. discolor)*; kiwakiwa *(B. fluviatile)*; kiokio *(B. novae-zelandiae)*.

Cyathea dealbata, ponga, silver fern: New Zealand's national icon occurs naturally mainly in lowland areas of North Island, and is distinguished by the pale silvery undersides of its fronds (though the name 'ponga' is commonly applied to tree ferns in general). The stipes or stems of the fronds are also covered in a whitish-silvery bloom. Ponga can grow to 10 metres with fronds up to 4 metres long, arching out like an enormous fountain. Though ponga is considered tough and tolerant of dryness, those planted on the Dune continue to struggle each summer: fronds die prematurely and new fronds may emerge small and distorted. They consume huge amounts of water, so their long-term survival will likely depend on how much tank water can be spared for them.

Cyathea medullaris, mamaku: several of this tallest of New Zealand tree ferns appeared naturally on the south-facing slope of the Dune, from spores that must already have been in the ground. This was surprising because they prefer wet conditions. A couple more were planted but they all struggle with increasing dryness and some, which had grown to 2 metres, have already died completely, leaving rough black trunks covered in shield-shaped scars where fronds have detached.

Dicksonia squarrosa, wheki: a fast-growing small tree fern reaching less than 6 metres; tolerant of full sun and dry conditions, but the three specimens on the south-facing slope survive rather than thrive.

Doodia australis, pukuku, rasp fern: low-growing tough dark green fronds emerge light red when young, and fade to yellow when old. Patches of *Doodia* were already present on the Dune. It is now spreading over open and lightly shaded areas, forming dense mats that protect surface soil and help to stabilise slopes, but it can prevent other small ground covers from establishing, and may need to be removed around the stems of young shrubs and trees to reduce competition for water and nutrients, until the saplings can root deeply enough to tap sources that *Doodia* roots cannot reach.

Microsorum pustulatum, kowaowao, hound's tongue fern: a bright, shiny green low-growing fern, its fronds arranged in wide, flat, irregularly shaped lobes. Kowaowao inhabits dryer sites. It has naturally established itself, presumably from wind-borne spores or from fragments of rhizome preserved beneath the surface, and is colonising one small shaded area on top of the Dune. Kowaowao is an opportunist: its green dark-scaled rhizomes can spread far and rapidly, and have to be removed when they home-in on the roots of other plants that are being selectively watered.

Pteris tremula, turawera, shaking brake fern, tender brake: occurring mainly in coastal North Island and adapted to drier sites, its wide feathery fronds end in a sharp triangular shape and grow to almost a metre, arching gracefully. Turawera is another fern that has naturally established on the Dune in isolated sites on both north and south slopes.

Rhopalostylis sapida, nikau: a tall palm of damp, lowland forest that can grow to 10 metres. Stiff, strongly ribbed, erect leaves can reach 3 metres in length, the leaflets along each stem up to a metre long. Nikau is extremely slow-growing and marginally suitable for the Dune, but a group of three small seedlings were planted in a shaded hollow that tends to collect moisture. So far they are growing well though their trunks are less than a metre high after 10 years of growth.

Schizarea dichotoma, comb fern: thin green stems or stipes of up to 30 cm, end in much divided narrow pinna or leaflets giving the appearance of a fragile comb or a long, splayed fork. A companion to kauri forests, the fern occurs mainly in the Far North and is not common. The one specimen on the Dune popped up of its own accord from beneath a climbing rose in the 'round garden'. A wise move – the rose is watered during summer.

Sticherus cunninghamii, waekura, umbrella fern: thin black wiry stems up to 30 cm long, bear narrow regular fronds, arching over the ground and branching in a fan formation resembling an umbrella. A more local imagery is given in another Māori name for this fern, 'tapuwae kotuku', 'footprint of the white heron'. Though adapted to drier sites and commonly colonises banks and forest edges, the patches of waekura on the Dune are not so comfortable as to colonise a wider area.

SOURCES AND FURTHER READING

Clarke, Alan, (2007) *The Great Sacred Forest of Tane: a natural pre-history of Aotearoa*, Reed Books

Coster, J., (1983) 'The Aupouri Sand Dunes Archaeological Study – an interim, report', *NZ Archaeological Association Newsletter*, Vol.26 No.3 pp174-191

Darwin, Charles, (1836) *The Voyage of the Beagle*, Marshall Cavendish Ltd 1987 edition

Eagle, Audrey, (2006) *Eagle's Complete Trees and Shrubs of New Zealand*, Vol.1 & 2, Te Papa Press

Evans, Alice, (1984) *Mount Camel Calling*, Hodder and Stoughton

Fenton, Francis Dart, 'Suggestions for a History of the Origin and Migrations of the Maori People', in The Pamphlet Collection of Sir Robert Stout, Vol. 52, online at Victoria University of Wellington Library

Hayward, Bruce W., (2017) *Out of the Ocean into the Fire*, Geoscience Society of New Zealand

Kereama Matire (Mrs M. Hoeft), (1968, republished 2019) *The Tail of the Fish*, Te Aupōuri Iwi Development Trust

King, Michael, (2003) *The Penguin History of New Zealand*, Penguin Books

Matthews, Caitlin & John, (1994) *Encyclopaedia of Celtic Wisdom*, Element

McGlone, Matt, S., Janet M. Wilmshurst and Helen M. Leach 'An Ecological and Historical Review of Bracken (*Pteridium esculetum*) in New Zealand and its Cultural Significance', *New Zealand Journal of Ecology*, Vol. 29, No. 2, (2005) pp.165–184 [Accessed online at: nzecology. org/nzje/2269.pdf]

Metcalf, Lawrie, (2003) *Ferns of New Zealand*, New Holland (NZ).

Northland Age and *Northern Luminary* (local newspapers with various subsequent name changes), from 1873 onwards, archives of the Far North Regional Museum, Te Atu, Kaitaia

Orbell, Margaret, (2003) *Birds of Aotearoa: a natural and cultural history*, Reed Books

Sale, E. V., (1981), *Historic Trails of the Far North*, Reed Books

Sale, E. V., (1985) *Forest on Sand: the Story of Aupouri State Forest*, New Zealand Forest Service

Simard, Suzanne, (2021) *Finding the Mother Tree: Discovering the Wisdom of the Forest,* Knopf

Sir Alfred Reed, (original publication 1972) *The Gumdiggers: The Story of Kauri Gum*, Bush Books

Sir Maui Pomare, Ed. James Cowan, (original publication 1930) *Legends of the Maori*, Vol. I & II, Southern Reprints (1987), accessible online at Victoria University of Wellington Library

Suzanne W. Simard, David A. Perry, Melonice D. Jones, David D. Myrold, Daniel M. Durall and Randy Molina, 'Net transfer of carbon between ectomycorrhizal tree species in the field', *Nature* 388 (1997) pp. 579-582

Wohlleben, Peter, (2017) *The Hidden Life of Trees*, William Collins

WEBSITES

These institutions all maintain accessible, easily searchable websites:

Department of Conservation, Te Papa Atawhai, conservation of New Zealand's natural and historical heritage, and encouragement of outdoor activities

Forest & Bird, Royal Forest and Bird Protection Society of New Zealand, an independent environmental organisation for the conservation of native flora and fauna

Ministry of Education, Te Tāhuhu O Te Mātaurangi, teaching resources for Te Reo Māori, history, mythology, environment, and all school subjects

Museum of New Zealand, Te Papa Tongarewa, Wellington, digital access to collections, publications, videos

New Zealand Birds Online, digital encyclopaedia of all birds found in New Zealand

New Zealand Geographic, interesting articles about native flora, fauna and landscape https://www.nzgeo.com/stories/paper-wasps-guests-or-pests/

Te Ara, Encyclopaedia of New Zealand, in English and Te Reo Māori, including sections on native flora and fauna

Turnbull Library Pictures, a broad collection of photographs, maps, drawings etc from the Alexander Turnbull Collection, including photographs of gum-digging and the kauri timber industry, online at the National Library, Auckland

ACKNOWLEDGEMENTS

As well as a nature memoir, *The Five Acre Forest* is also a celebration of place – of one small, specific place – but the underlying philosophy is universal, and I wanted to make the narrative accessible to be enjoyed by anyone, anywhere. To that end, I found discerning folk in five countries to read and make editorial comments on the whole text. They were generous in their suggestions and encouragement, and I give my heartfelt thanks to: Chris Cotman, Kenneth Glazier, Nick Nicholson, Karen Phillips, Valerie Poore, Nicola Robb, Avril Silk, Marie-Hélène Thomas, and Margaret Warburton.

I am also grateful to those who read and advised on specific parts of the text, provided specialist information, aided me in accessing research, or offered the enthusiasm and expectation that kept me going: Elaine Aldred, Amy Gigi Alexander, Steve Amon, Dr Anne Marie D'arcy, Mary Daun, Kevin Matthews, Liz Meek, and Helen and Stephen Yuretich. And this is a good place to express my appreciation of Andy Gay, whose practical assistance on the Dune has lightened my workload over recent years.

We live in an era where social media is a significant part of our connectedness to the world. With care, it is a source for good, and a special mention is due for all of the Twitter tree-people, nature lovers, conservationists, and naturalists from all corners of the world who have consistently inspired me to share the story of the *Five Acre Forest*, and who respond with spontaneous generosity to my postings on the trees, creatures and landscape around me. You are too numerous to name individually, but you all know who you are.

And of course, after all the feedback, checking and cross-checking, any remaining errors are my own.